MW00929546

Through The Woods

By

MARGIE MACK

Copyright © 2014 Margie Mack

All rights reserved.

ISBN: 1496067215

ISBN 13: 9781496067210

Dedication

Thank you, Grandma Cleo and Grandpa Bill. You gave me a home where there was none, laughter when I'd cried so many, many tears, and most of all, you never told me no. You told me to believe in the magic of the world, and for this I do.

Love, Margie

The sun it crept across the room
With splendor everywhere
The warmth it fell upon my face
Drew colors in my hair
All objects sitting in this room
The ominous, the meek
At one time or another
With the sun played hide and seek
Margie

INTRODUCTION

*G*rowing up is an adventure, regardless of where you are or who you live with. For me, growing up was magical. I was lucky to be raised by my grandparents Bill and Cleo Mauer. They were, of course, from an entirely different generation, but what was good for them fifty years before, they felt was good enough for me. I still sit and try to will myself back to those days of learning to be a human being, because that was what they strived to help me do. They worked together to help form my young mind into believing that there was mystery to life, that magic was all around me, and most importantly, that I was loved by them. My grandparents looked at raising me as a second chance of sorts. What they didn't do right with my mother, they would do better with me.

When fate changed their lives in such a drastic way, requiring them to raise me, they took that change in stride, calmly and peacefully. My mother needed to leave, and I am sure that was a hard thing for them to allow—but allow they did. They made it possible for her to go to work and live in Chicago, so that the life she was destined to live would be within her grasp and not fifty miles away in a small suburb of McHenry, Illinois, called Colby Point. Grandpa's sisters— my aunts Lily, Dula, and Sylvia—lived at the end of that narrow, dirt road, and Bill and Cleo followed. A handful of other family members were scattered throughout the neighborhood.

Our one-story house was pink, and it had a crawlspace and an attic. That crawlspace held its dark and mysterious secrets under the trapdoor in the small hall closet. The attic door was in the garage, and there was no way I could ever be able to climb up there and poke around at the boxes that Grandpa kept up there. The house was so small that if you took five adults and had them stand with their arms outstretched hand-to-hand, they would span the entire length of our home. It consisted of two bedrooms, one bathroom, a kitchen, and a living room. But it was a palace to me, and I loved the way I felt safe and wanted in their home.

I am haunted by the memories and the lessons that I experienced growing up, and I still go back there and sit at the end of the road. I look around at that place that looked so big to me, and I am shocked that it still looks big, even though I have changed. Somehow the house has managed to maintain the same atmosphere. The trees have grown, the house is now a different color, but if I stand really still, the spirits of Cleo and Bill are all around it. I know that if I touch that house, it can help me find myself. I have not had the nerve to do that yet, but I will someday before it is gone.

There was one way in and one way out on Colby Point Road. Most the inhabitants were summer dwellers. My Grandpa Bill and his sisters, Lilly, Silvia and Dula had originally bought a summer home there back in the 1930s when my mother was small. Great-grandparents and aunts and uncles and cousins all came to the first house. Then one by one, they scattered to the city, and Colby Point became a "remember when" sort of place.

When Mother was young, she and my grandparents enjoyed the city, and my mother perfected her craft. She wove her way through the city and became known as a blind but beautiful, very talented, jazz pianist. Mom always had gentlemen interested in her, but one day a big, dark-haired man by the name of Jack came into the lounge where she was playing. One thing led to another, and they fell in love. After my parents were married and had me, though, the storms began and never ended. Grandpa decided that the farther away he moved his family—Mother included—the better, so he bought the lot across the street from his sisters and moved us as far away from Chicago that he could go. Five thousand dollars got the house built, and the four of us moved out to the end of the world. But my mother was slowly dying out there in Colby Point. One day, a relative of my grandfather came to visit us. He could see what was happening, so he convinced my grandparents that the best place for my mother was in the city, and the best place for me was with them.

The rest is history for the family, except for me. It is my past, present, and my future. I cannot let this memory leave me. When I need peace, I close my eyes and think of the full and majestic life I had with Grandma Cleo and Grandpa Bill. They gave my mother the freedom to work and live her life because she knew I was safe, and that was all that mattered. So we settled down to a routine, and I learned how to be a human.

I still smile when I hear my grandfather's words: "Margie"—he would say—"I do believe that you are turning into a human right before my eyes." I am so glad that he told me that, because I have always felt a part of the human race.

So now, I am going to take you back with me to my world as a little girl. Grandma Cleo was in a wheelchair with multiple sclerosis, and Grandpa Bill had this house built especially for her. Wide doorways, smooth floors, and a huge picture window that was low and wide so that when Grandma would wheel herself to the window, she was able to see the beauty that he tried to give to her. In our yard there were trees of all kinds and birds and deer...for us, the seasons came and went, with each season more bountiful and beautiful than the last.

What happened to me in Colby Point helped keep my imagination and my faith alive. Not the type of faith that is a routine church faith, but the kind of faith that allows me to say "I believe" and know it is true even if I do not see it, and that if there is a mystery that I cannot solve, then it is okay that it not be solved. The most complete feeling is to be able to sit and wonder why and then accept that there is no logical reason for it to be—and that, my friends, is the magic that I write about in my stories.

Everything that I present to you really happened to me. I write it as I remember it, whether I am five years old or fifty. The people in my stories are the same people who desired for the beautiful magic of Colby Point to continue on forever. And just like me, they had hope.

So come and sit a while. Visit my world, my home, my family—and allow these stories shape the ones that you love, the hands that you hold near to you, because what would our world be without magic?

TABLE OF CONTENTS

Chapter One

COLBY POINT

There is a place where I once lived and ran among the trees.
The thistle and the sweet grass grew wild around my knees.
And as I lay upon the ground while Mother Earth did turn,
The relentless rays of brightest sun, upon my skin did burn.
There was so much to look at, each place a secret told.
For each one I discovered, another one unfolds.
Did you know bees made love at dawn? Where honey does exist?
They drink upon the nectar that's thick among the mist.
And if I can, I reach my hand into that secret place.
The telltale signs of honey that shine upon my face.
Now when that's done, my cooling place, I'll walk along the shore.
Fox River travels eagerly, with shells and rocks and more.
With stolen things from place to place, it travels now downstream.
I lay along Fox lazily it's warm, and I do dream
Of all the places I love best, the valleys and the trees,
My friends the squirrel and bobolinks, and fuzzy, busy bees.
The road it winds along the earth from where it does begin.
Each turn so different from the next, its pattern like snakeskin.
Across the lawn and through the field, into the trees I creep.

A mystery there with magic, a hiding place I'll keep.
And as I sit, my friends do come, the rabbit and the deer.
Now hide with them; alone are we, for man won't find us here.
Thank you, Lord, for this great gift of nature that I've seen.
For Colby Point is calling now, if only in my dreams.

❦

When I was two-and-a-half years old, my mother and father separated and eventually divorced. My mom was legally blind with only partial sight, and my father needed to roam about the country. It's funny that when you are a child, you picture your parents in such a way that their flaws do not matter. I am sure that none of us wanted a broken family—we'd much rather prefer the families we watched on the TV set. The people on *Father Knows Best, The Donna Reed Show,* and *The Andy Griffith Show* were my role models for what I wanted in parents. But when life handed us a bowl of lemons we learned how to make lemonade, as Grandma Cleo always said.

Grandpa Bill had our lives pretty well planned out. The move to the small suburb of McHenry, Illinois, was such a drastic one that it took Grandma and my mother by surprise. Grandpa was fine with the fact that the four of us all shared a house that was only about nine-hundred square feet, because the outside was endless.

After six months of living with us there, my mother would be gone, and some of the tension would leave with her. But the tears—my tears—were left behind. Being so young, I was somewhat content to be with my grandparents. They made me feel so safe and so loved.

Grandpa had painted our new house pink! I thought that he did it for me, but what actually happened was that he tried to get a pale red but added turpentine to the paint to thin it out. When it was all done, it dried pink! The window in the front room was almost as big as the entire wall, and the doors all were extra wide. Grandma had multiple sclerosis and was in a wheelchair. Were they prepared to raise a two-and-a-half-year-old? Not really. But could they do it? You bet they could!

As I became aware of who I was and where I was, my imagination began to grow. There were limits set in place, and I quickly learned that I could not go past the edge of the lawn on our huge lot. I learned that I always had to at least try Grandma's new foods, as eating hadn't been one of my strong points. But most of all, I knew that I could pretty much do whatever I wanted as long as I promised to discuss it first and not get hurt. So picture this—a gravel road that had two houses on one side and twelve on the other. The two houses belonged to my grandparents and my aunt Malita. Aunt Malita was a widow who was painfully thin, loved to smoke, and sucked on peppermints.

Aunt Malita was a good person, but she was deaf as a doornail and also very cheap. She would say to me, "Save your pennies for a rainy day, Margie, because when there is a storm, you may need protection." For the life of me I could not figure out how I could make pennies protect me from the rain. I saved them, nevertheless, but occasionally broke down and cashed them in for a Hostess cupcake.

Directly across the street from our house lived my aunts Sylvia, Dula, and Lily. They were three spinster aunts who had a love for organization. They were my grandpa Bill's older sisters. Grandpa had four sisters and one brother. Irma lived in Chicago with her husband Lawrence, and Uncle Elmer lived across the creek from our tiny home with his crazy wife, Aunt Louise. (I wasn't supposed to say it then, but I will say it now.) She was crazier than a bedbug, trusting no one except for me. Says a lot for my innocence back then, right?

Anyway, the houses that were not occupied by family were either permanent dwellers or summer vacation people. All in all, life in Colby Point was slow and easy, and there was a softness about it. There were no surprises except when the milkman got sick and his wife showed up delivering the milk, eggs, and butter. Or when the storm was so bad that a huge tree fell across the road, and since there was only one way in and one way out, all the men and Aunt Sylvia went down to where it had fallen, cut it up, and pulled it out of the way. What was nice was that they didn't leave it on the side of the road to rot, but instead, they cut it up and everyone took some of that majestic tree home to use for their fireplaces or their gardens. Nothing was wasted there.

I think that I was placed out there at the end of the road because life was preparing me to learn some lessons that would place in me a stubborn conviction that everything happens for a reason, and that there is magic in everything! Somewhere inside every problem and every celebration there is the miracle of magic waiting to be acknowledged. As I grew older, I locked away in my heart the miracles and magic of my childhood to make sure that I'd remember them all my life.

There was plenty of danger at Colby Point, though, as the Fox River was not a river to be ignored. It ran fast in the winter and spring, white and frozen yet fast and furious below the ice, simply teasing and winking at you as it traveled from nowhere to somewhere. Summer and fall, well, those were the times when the Fox was friendly and inviting. Fish would wait patiently as horseflies lingered dangerously close to the surface, never realizing that they were about to be nice fat morsels for the river carp that hid below.

The movement of the water was methodical yet soft, and I swear I could be up at the house, playing in the coolness of our garage, and I would hear the river calling to me. "Margie," it murmured. "Margie! Come along to the river and dip your toes." Over and over it would call, until I would drop my dolls and yell to my grandparents that I was going to the river for a dip. I'd strip off all my clothes except my shorts as I ran gingerly across the pea-gravel road. Tinkerbell, my toy fox terrier pup, would run alongside, nipping at my feet and making the run over the gravel road difficult.

Grandpa would shout, "You stay in the shallow end, you hear? And hey, watch out for those water moccasins—they're nesting now, and they will be a-biting!" And for just a moment, I would hesitate...and then that little bit of fear would disappear, and I was in my river, my lazily warm and gentle river with her golden jewels shining at me from below. I would lie on my back and float and just let the current take me away, but I never let myself drift past Boldt's pier.

Back near the shore, the minnows would come near me and nibble on my toes. That always made me laugh. After about an hour, as I became all pruned-up, I would feel a stinging sensation and know that those darn bloodsuckers had gotten into my shorts again.

"Time to leave," I'd call to Tinkerbell. Once back at the house, I would take the water hose and wash off the muck from the river, then take off my shorts. Grandpa would already have the salt, as he could see bloodsuckers all over my behind.

Shaking his head he would say, "I told you not to sit on the bottom of that river so long. You're gonna get faint if you keep doin' that, y'hear me?"

"Yes, Grandpa. I promise not to do it again," I'd say as I crossed my fingers on both hands. We both knew that I would never stay out of the river.

Grandma would have a grape-jam sandwich with chips and a Hostess cupcake waiting for me for lunch, and after that I would find a nice, cool place to take a nap as the whole house would become quiet.

Yes, life in Colby Point was good to me. At times though, some things were hard to understand, but Grandma and Grandpa always found a way to help me understand. They taught me to change the things I could and to accept the things that I couldn't.

The cornfield behind my house led to a valley where my imagination turned me into "Wildfire," a beautiful black horse who lived and ran wild in the fields. Along the valley was a hill where I made a fort, and there was a creek that wound around and around and back near my house. My teenage neighbor, Joey Fino, taught me to fish in that creek. I had my first crush on Joey, and I just knew that someday when I was all grown up, he would take me away and marry me and we would have a family of our own.

There was a bridge crossing that creek that connected the two Colby Point roads. My best friend Peggy Walker was there on the other side every summer with her family. The DeMarcos, the

Adimites, and Uncle Elmer, Aunt Louise, and my cousins Ronnie and Lindalu lived on that side of the creek. Lindalu was like the big sister I never had. When she could, she watched over me, and I liked that feeling. It was nice.

I am sure that you are beginning to get the feeling of what my world was like by now. The tiny homes at night were aglow with amber lights, and the sound of laughter could be heard trickling down the road, as everyone had their windows open in the summertime. The stars were brightest in winter though, because so many of our neighbors were gone. Without the lights shining in the little homes, it was darker in Colby Point than anywhere else in the world, I swear! And it was all mine.

One particularly hot summer night, I just couldn't sleep. It was so hot, but Grandma was always cold and the windows were not allowed to be open too much at night. So that night, I was lying on the living room floor with my blanket and pillow, and I felt like I was being cooked alive. Tinkerbell was lying on the cool linoleum floor on her belly but continued to pant. I waited until I couldn't stand it any longer, then I opened the front door and slipped out into the starlit night. I took my blanket and pillow and my dog and went outside to sleep. Birds kept the mosquito population low by eating most of them, and the grass that I was going to lay on was thick and cool alongside of the house.

I can still remember that night—the coolness of the air and the sound of the night train. I felt safe and so alive. The stars gave me the wonderment of the world as the night train called to me, and I knew at that moment that my small life wasn't small at all. I mattered and I had all of this around me. The stars, the trees, the river, and the night train...they were all mine, and they are still mine today. Colby Point will be my home forever.

Chapter Two

THE CHRISTMAS WISH

If just one wish I did possess, I'd place it in your hand;
I'd tell you how I spent the rest and hope you'd understand.
A wish is something that can be the best and worst of me.
For if a wish is used for wrong, the wish itself won't last too long.
I took this wish and opened it and guessed what it beheld.
The rhyme and reason didn't fit, I dropped it and it fell.
But just before it smashed and shattered, the core released its wings.
A sound that came across so still, it sang of different things.
This wish is growing from within and has a life to bare.
It slowly wraps around your heart and brings more wishes there.
So guard each wish that you now hold, won't wither,
burn, or gather cold,
Instead of ice the fire's glow, the wish your heart will truly know.

∾

*I*t was December 1, 1958, three weeks before Christmas, and Colby Point seemed emptier than usual. Most residents left when summer was gone, but we'd always had a few neighbors who would stick out the winter weather. This year was different. Even my best friend Peggy Walker and her family had gone back to their city home. So I had to rely on my grandparents and my four aunts to keep me busy. At four and a half years old, I wasn't a bad child, I was just imaginative and full of questions. Being raised with grandparents that were a whole generation removed from me gave me a whole different scope on life. I acted older than I was. I understood things that I really shouldn't have had to and being around grownups most of the time made me much more confident than kids my age.

My grandparents made sure that every day of the week had a schedule of some sort. Mondays were for cleaning, and we each had our chores to do. On Tuesdays, we did the laundry. I loved Wednesdays because I got to go to Crystal Lake with my grandpa to do the shopping for the week. On Thursdays, Aunts Dula, Lily, Sylvia, and Malita played cards. I was allowed to watch as long as I didn't blurt out their hidden cards. Fridays were for reading or writing letters. Weekends were for playtime and church. So you can see, as a little girl I was happy with the business of our lives. I was five, but there was no kindergarten in Prairie Grove School, so school didn't start for me for another whole year.

Church was special because I was able to go off with my aunts without my grandparents. They trusted me to go to my class and know my lessons from the week before. Pastor Neating had two sons, Teddy and Linus. I loved to watch Teddy and Linus come in with their mom and then settle down for the first part of church that we were allowed to attend. They were a family, and it felt good to see that because that is what I wanted more than anything—a mother and a father. Don't get me wrong: I loved Grandma and Grandpa, but it seemed that something was not complete in me. I didn't dwell on it too much and I never was sad; I was just happy to see that my friends had something that I wanted for myself. I also knew that someday I would have my own home filled with the laughter of children.

Every Sunday, weather permitting; I got dressed up in my Sunday-best clothes. Church in the summertime was hard because all I wanted to do was run barefoot across the grass to the Fox River. So I welcomed the winter time, as it calmed me down. I felt grown up in my Sunday dress, patent leather shoes, and white rabbit-fur muff to keep my hands warm. Aunt Dula would walk across the road and make sure I was ready, then together Aunts Sylvia, Lily, Dula, and I would take the long ride to St. John's Lutheran Church in Island Lake. The drive into Island Lake was slow but always full of surprises. Aunt Dula and I always sat in the backseat as Aunt Sylvia drove. Aunt Lily was her copilot. Aunt Dula made it a game for me as we tried to guess what the other one saw.

The Sunday two weeks before Christmas that year was especially exciting for me. Pastor Neating had announced a contest for wishes. He wanted to know from his parishioners if they had a wish that they would like fulfilled for Christmas, or maybe they knew of someone else that had a need that would help make their Christmas a little brighter. I had given this request a lot of thought, and I was excited because I had the perfect wish for the perfect people! Finally, Sunday morning was here, and Grandma Cleo was trying her best to help me get ready for church. Grandpa Bill never left Grandma for too long, so going to church for them was not something that they could accomplish.

"What is up with you?" Grandma asked. "Why are you so darned fidgety?"

I felt as if I was bursting inside and wanted to tell Grandma all about the wish but decided not to as it might not come true. Looking around for a quick diversion I said, "Nothing, Grandma....Umm, it's my shoes. They feel too tight, that's all." I made sure that I crossed my fingers behind my back for telling a fib. "I just want to hurry to church so I will get a good seat in the front so I can see everything, that's all."

Grandpa was listening while shaving and said, "Well you can't put the cart before the horse—after all you have to ride with the aunts, and you know how slow they drive. You might as well just settle down."

Grandma had a way of looking at me when she thought that I was hiding something from her. It always made me feel uneasy. I wanted to avoid that, so as soon as my dress was buttoned up and Grandma had given me a nod of approval, I ran to the front room. I grabbed my hat, coat, Bible, and winter muff and yelled, "I ain't waiting for Aunt Dula. I want to get a good seat."

Grandpa said something as I slammed the front door. Tinkerbell started barking, but I was determined to get everyone to hurry up! My patent leather shoes made the newly fallen snow under my feet feel like ice on the Fox River, so I slid all the way down our driveway and right into Aunt Dula's stomach!

"Here! Here now, you have to slow down," Aunt Sylvia said as she caught my arm before I fell on Aunt Dula's feet. "You'll be all tuckered out before we even get to church." She laughed as she opened the front door for Aunt Lily. Aunt Lily was the keeper of the candy, and she eyed me as if to say that if I was real good, she'd have a treat for me. I climbed into the generous backseat of their brand new Buick and settled down for a ride of talking and singing and a little bit of family gossip. Our ride was long to the small church in Island Lake, and when we arrived, it was busy with families all coming together for a day of prayer and celebration.

Aunt Sylvia hadn't even turned the car off before I was opening the door and darting past people so that I could get to the first pew at the front of the church. Aunt Dula was a greeter, so she took her place at the door. Aunt Lily went to the choir, and Aunt Sylvia settled into her seat at the back where I was supposed to be. I turned around and waved at her. She looked puzzled at my seat choice, but it didn't matter. I wanted the service to begin so that I could tell Pastor Neating about my wish. The music began and after singing "Onward Christian Soldiers," everyone was seated. Pastor Neating seemed to take a particularly long time this Sunday talking about doing unto others as you would have them do unto to you. After the very last "amen," he finally began to talk about the Christmas wish.

"As most of you know, we do have parishioners at St. John's Lutheran Church who are having a hard time at this time of year. They may be out of work or have an illness or perhaps have lost a loved one. Today, we have five members who want to ask for their

Christmas wish to be granted. Remember, this is the time when we need to look at how we can help others. So...without further ado, let's begin shall we?"

I watched and listened as, one by one, several adults came forward and talked about their needs and wishes for the holiday season. I paid attention to what the others said as I wanted to make sure that my wish was different from anyone else's. After the fourth person was done and just before Pastor Neating said that it was time for the last person to come up, I stood up and began to straighten my Christmas dress. This seemed to get everyone's attention, including Aunt Sylvia. She seemed to be nervous at my standing up and was trying to get my attention. So was Aunt Lily, who was sitting across from me in the choir. Finally I heard my name, and I walked bravely up to the pulpit. Pastor Neating brought a stepstool for me to stand on, and then I waited for him to have a seat before I began.

"My name is Margie Mauer Reiling, and I go to this church. I come every week with Aunt Dula, Aunt Lily, and Aunt Sylvia. I have to leave Grandma Cleo and Grandpa Bill at home." I waved to my aunts, and the entire congregation turned around to see them blushing in their seats.

"My Christmas wish is for my grandma and grandpa to have church come to them. Since Grandpa can't leave Grandma alone because Grandma can't walk, it sure would be nice if you all came for a visit and surprised them. We have a small house, but Grandma bakes really good sugar cookies. Right, Pastor Neating? I know you like them because you always have at least two when you come to visit Grandma and pray with her." All heads turned to the back of the room where Pastor Neating smiled and waved sheepishly while the rest of the congregation chuckled softly.

"So if you choose my wish, we will be ready, but it has to be a surprise because that is how Christmas wishes come true, right?" I got down and walked to the back of the church. I could feel eyes on me, and I also saw lots of smiling and whispering going on. The ride home was a silent one, and I couldn't understand why Aunt Lily did nothing but sniffle and Aunt Dula hugged herself tightly while Aunt Sylvia tried to find some Christmas music on the radio. Once at home again, the hardest thing for me was not to tell Grandma what I had done. As the days crept along, Grandma kept her eye on me and every once in a while I could hear her whispering to Grandpa about what I was up to.

Finally, Christmas arrived, and I woke up to the smell of Grandpa's bacon cooking on the small white stove.

I jumped out of bed shouting, "Merry Christmas!" to my family.

"Merry Christmas to you," answered Grandma and Grandpa together. "Did you see the presents that Santa Claus left for you under the tree?"

I was busy getting dressed and hollered, "Not yet, Grandma, but I will." I could hear Grandma telling Grandpa how it was strange that I was taking time to get dressed, because I usually made a beeline right to the gifts. My mother had come for a visit, and she had brought me a beautiful, blue taffeta dress. I was going to wear it to Sunday morning church. That wasn't for hours yet, but I decided to dress up now, just in case my wish came true.

I walked into the kitchen and did a little twirl to let them see that I was dressed and as pretty as I could be for them. I loved them so much.

But then Grandma said, "You're not going to church today, honey. We got a call from Pastor Neating, and he said church wasn't going to have services today. You can get changed into something more comfortable."

I guess I didn't looked surprised or happy when I replied, "But there has to be church today. There are wishes to come true!" I went over to the big, overstuffed, red chair that was in the middle of the front window. Tinkerbell and I sat there looking out the window, waiting for the big surprise to begin. I refused to let the tears fall or for doubt to enter in.

Grandpa came in with a plate of toast and bacon for me and said, "I'm not sure what you're waitin' on, honey, but after you eat this breakfast, how 'bout we open the presents that Santa left you?"

I was too excited to eat, so I set the plate down and Tinker began to help herself. That made Grandma angry. About thirty minutes went by, but I still refused to budge. Finally, Grandpa came into the living room and started talking to me about all the fine gifts that there were. Then he looked out the window and saw a steady stream of cars coming down the road to our house. Grandpa stood for a good five minutes, watching as car after car came to our driveway and began to park all over the lawn. People got out of their cars carrying food and gifts, and then he saw Pastor Neating.

Scratching his head, he shouted, "Cleo, you're not going to believe this, but I think the whole dang church is on our front lawn." Then he turned to me and asked, "Margie, what did you do?"

I allowed the tears to fall as I laughed and spun around and said, "I knew my wish would come true—I knew it! I wished that since you and Grandma could never go to church, that church would come to you, and it did. Don't you see, my wish did come true!" I wanted to be the one to greet our visitors, so I ran and opened the front door. Grandpa and Grandma sat quietly watching the miracle unfold.

"I can't believe that our little Margie did this for us," Grandpa said to Grandma Cleo.

Grandma Cleo smiled and said, "I do, because—you see, Bill, when Margie wishes, she usually gets what she wants. We taught her that, you and me, right? But there's only one problem I can foresee, Bill."

"What's that Cleo?"

"I don't think we have enough coffee cups to go around."

The door opened up and Pastor Neating had me in his arms. "Bill, Cleo. I hope you will say that this is all right. When the church heard your granddaughter's wish, we couldn't think of any other wish to grant. So sit back and enjoy this visit. Because of your granddaughter's love for you, this was the best present that we could have ever given."

That Christmas Sunday was a grand day for the Mauer family. We sang songs of love and hope and faith, and we had each other. As the choir sang "Silent Night," I realized that I had gotten the best thing in the world for Christmas.

I got my wish.

Chapter Three

THE CHRISTMAS ANGEL

Cold and clear with icy blue, the taste it burns my tongue,
Snowflakes fall with gentle ease, our winter has begun.
Now, there are places right nearby that man has never seen,
But Grandpa and little Tinkerbell, they know what I mean.
In winter, silence is a shout that deafens noisy ears,
The rabbit and the skittish grouse find it strangely queer
That I would cherish untouched snow for pure it will remain,
For Colby Point in winter's night will always stay the same.

✺

I was five years old in 1959, and I was eagerly waiting for the time when our street would be quiet. Don't get me wrong— having all the neighbors and family around helped make the days that were otherwise filled with just my own imagination go by quicker. I would fall into bed exhausted, dream all night long, and then wake up to be as tired as I was when I first fell into bed. The school that I would attend had no kindergarten, just first grade through seventh and I loved the joyful chaos at Prairie Grove School. Making friends was easy but everyone lived so far away that I had to rely on my own imagination to get me through most of days.

Aunts Sylvia, Dula, Lily, and Malita had decided to take a month-long cruise, so we wouldn't see them again until after January. Aunt Malita never went away, and it was going to be strange not to have the extra person to visit. Going to her house gave me a bit of freedom from the small home that we shared. I would walk next door and knock on her door, and Aunt Malita would be busy sucking on hard peppermint candy and smoking cigarettes. She was hard of hearing, so we would watch *The Price Is Right* at the loudest volume the television set could go. Aunt Malita was very cheap and she was stick thin no matter how much she ate. She always let me know that she had just enough food for her. I would say, "I'm not hungry for food, just some other people to talk to."

I remember the day they left for the cruise. I'd been looking out our huge picture window, watching the four of them drive away in the shiny, red Buick that Aunt Sylvia had just bought from Colby Auto. They had announced that if the snow was heavier this year, they wouldn't even be back until spring.

My aunts had left their house keys with Grandpa Bill so he could check on their houses if he needed to. Even as young as I was, when everyone in our house was supposed to be resting, I would often sneak out and walk to Aunt Malita's house. Once inside, I would just stand there, taking in the items that were carefully placed in the rooms. I missed my aunts being home, but it felt very grown up to have this time to myself.

One afternoon, Grandma decided to take a nap. Because she was in a wheelchair and could not get out and go lie down on her bed she would lay her head down on her pillow on the kitchen table.

I saw that Grandpa was already asleep in his room. Tinkerbell was curled up next to him, seemingly without a care in the world.

Grandma had recently finished reading a story to me about an angel who came to a town that was having all sorts of trouble. It was a story about how a young girl would go outside and talk to the sky as if someone was listening. Every time she did this, out of nowhere, an angel would appear. Only the girl could see the angel, and at first her family thought she was telling fibs—but then suddenly, the prayers that were being said were answered, and life became great for that whole lonely town. I wondered how difficult it must be to not know what was going to happen. My life was safe and secure, and I never felt unsure of who or where I was because I knew that it was the way it was supposed to be.

After Grandma read me that story, I decided that I was going to start to talk to the angels too. Grandma had such great faith in the unknown that when we would say our prayers together at night, I could somehow feel that the angels were with us in that little pink house at the end of the gravel road. Knowing that there was a being or an energy that was greater than me made me feel important. Not in a conceited way, but in a more grown-up way. It was my time of knowing that I had a purpose and that no matter what went wrong, someone was watching out for me.

Grandma always told me, "tears at night, joy in the morning," whenever I was worried about something. So I got my boots, hat, and coat on and snuck out the front door into the cold winter's afternoon. I walked to the end of the driveway and looked down our street. Only three other homes were occupied this winter, and their lights were just beginning to shine in the darkening sky. Turning toward the river, I walked down past the aunts' deserted house. The Fox River wasn't frozen yet, and it was running fast. It was so quiet outside in the cold air that I finally felt relaxed enough to let out a sigh.

"It is good to have you to myself." I said aloud. No one was around, and even at this young age, I found that talking to the Fox River or the trees or the sky above with its bright stars was therapeutic for me. I didn't feel alone at all, because I felt that I was the caretaker of this land.

I walked for about an hour between our home and the aunts' house. I decided that the snow was the deepest in the back where our lot met up with the cornfield. I centered my feet and held my arms out straight by my sides. Then I held my breath and allowed my body to fall back, flat onto the snow. As I hit the ground, all the air came out of me really quick. I then proceeded to make a snow angel. It was great fun, and I figured that if I made it for all the stars to see, maybe our guardian angel would look down on us and keep us safe from harm.

The light at the back of the house went off and on a few times, and that was my signal to come in for supper. I stood up careful-like and hopped away from the snow angel so I wouldn't ruin it. I was very pleased with it and waved at the angel as I ran to the house. It was warm in the kitchen, and the bright hurricane lamp lit the yellow walls so they seemed more gold than yellow. Grandma had been cooking all day and had made my favorite white bean soup with homemade bread. She had made a whole bunch of cupcakes with chocolate frosting, too, which was unusual. I wondered to myself if she was expecting company. Grandma liked to save the big portions of sweets for when Pastor Neating came by for a visit. He could never eat just one and always managed to grab a couple for the long ride back to the church.

Grandpa had been out in the backyard, making sure that our furnace would stay lit. It had gone out a few times over the past week, and with the snowstorm coming tonight, he made sure that the path was clear to the oil flue and that the flue itself was open.

"Bill, are you coming in for supper?" Grandma sounded a bit put-out, and I looked at her and saw that she seemed worried about something.

"Are you mad about something, Grandma," I asked timidly. Grandpa walked in at that precise moment and answered before she could open her mouth.

"She ain't mad, she's just worried that she will freeze to death!" His hands were red from the cold night air and black from the oil flue. He was smiling, and all of a sudden Grandma's frown turned upside down, and she was laughing with him. All I could think to myself was that grownups were so confusing.

"You get yourself cleaned up, Bill Mauer, before you starve to death!" Now Grandpa Bill was very thin—so thin that I could feel his hip bones when I would climb up on his lap for our evening story. Grandpa told me that he was thin from the years he was away in the war overseas. It all sounded very dangerous as he told his stories of living in the woods to avoid the enemy that we were fighting. I sure was glad I lived in times where we didn't have to look for our food or sleep outdoors during the winter months.

Soon enough, we all settled into our spots for dinner—Grandma on the right side of the small table, Grandpa on the stool that had a bright red oilcloth cover on it on the left side, and I was in the middle on my favorite kitchen chair. It had a nice, soft chair pad that Grandma had made for me with a beautiful horse on it. Tinkerbell was at my feet, waiting patiently for me to drop a few morsels for her to enjoy. But then, just as we finished with supper and Grandma pulled out the cupcakes for dessert, the lights in our house went off and on a few times. We all froze as we waited and hoped that it would just stay on. Grandma reached into the drawer under our phone, and pulled out a box of matches. Grandpa got up and grabbed the hurricane lamps from the living room and set them on the table. He also gathered the flashlights we had. Time passed, and the furnace kept running, and we felt safe for another night. But none of us were in the mood for dessert, so we went to bed.

Yes, my life was good with Cleo and Bill Mauer. Every evening as we ate, one of them would begin a story about their lives growing up and the adventures that they had experienced. What was truly great to hear was that, regardless of what adversity hit them, they would always somehow overcome the problem and move on. Time stood still for me when I was a young girl. Dinner wasn't hurried as it was our time to get to know each other, as Grandpa always said. I sit here now and long for those times—just to go back, just once, to hear and see and smell the house that built me. To listen to Billie Holiday's "I'll be Seeing You."

As Christmas drew nearer, I thought about all that I had and about how I didn't feel the need to be afraid of things. I had my dog Tinkerbell, Grandma and Grandpa, and a very active imagination.

I never lacked for things to do. I wrote stories, painted, practiced the piano that Grandma was teaching me, and I loved to work with clay.

I imagined that I had a mysterious magical life outside with the animals that lived in the forest around me. The wild forest and the river seemed to change their appearance with every season. There were squirrels, deer, and rabbits that came regularly to our yard to be fed. Grandpa put out a saltlick for them, because that saltlick kept up their appetite. The trees were generous this year. There were trees with hard, red berries that had lived through the first frost. Other trees had huge brown pinecones, and others, small dark acorns lined up with their hats on. We had wild mistletoe and a huge cactus that bloomed only at Christmas time.

I had a variety of things to be creative with while I made the Christmas presents I would give away. Each year beginning in November, Grandma would begin working on her Christmas cards. Having only one hand that worked slowed her down, so as I got older, I helped her stuff the cards with either pictures or a poem that she had wanted to share. I am proud to say that I have carried on the tradition for fifty years now. I send about a hundred and fifty cards a year to friends and family.

Through the winter, Grandpa would work on his car, keep our water running in the freezing weather, manage to keep our old oil furnace working, and take care of every living thing that came down our street, whether it was animal or human. Everyone knew him and loved him. Bob Ferguson, our mailman, often stopped in for a cup of coffee, as did the milkman Tom Walker and also Sheriff Joe Fino. I felt important and safe, knowing that three important men in the community would come and visit my grandparents. I really think it was Grandma's cupcakes that brought them there. I would sit for hours when we had visitors such as these and listen to their stories about the outside world that I had not had time to experience yet. It made life intriguing for me; in fact, life became an addiction of sorts, as I wanted to be part of everything I could.

We were known as a "safe" house in those days, and we were proud of it. Strangers were not to be feared but were rather a gift to us, because they brought us news from the outside world that we didn't often get a chance to see.

This particular Christmas season, Grandpa was having a harder time than usual with the furnace. He was outside working on it a lot, and after being outside in the sub-zero cold weather, he would finally have to give up and come inside to warm up a bit. So one night, Grandpa was bothered because he knew that the weekend would soon be here, and there weren't any neighbors or people expected for a few days in our neck of the woods. He was concerned that Grandma and I would get sick if the furnace continued to break down and the house got too cold. So while the furnace was running, Grandma and I made soup and a sweet potato pie for dinner. Grandpa came in, and I could hear him muttering under his breath to himself.

"What's wrong," I asked.

"Oh, I was just talkin' to God," Grandpa said. "Asking him to please help me figure out a way to keep that old furnace running until Monday, so I can get a furnace man out here for help...that's all."

Grandma had dinner all ready for us, but just as we sat down to eat, the room went dark and the furnace went off again. Grandpa got up and found all the hurricane lanterns and took out his matches and lit them.

"While the food is still hot, Bill, sit down and eat some." Grandma said. "We will think of something, I am sure of it."

Grandpa didn't say anything at all, he just pushed his food away and walked into the other room and sat down. Grandma motioned for me to be quiet, and we sat there eating our supper. He was worried because if he couldn't keep the furnace lit, we could freeze to death. With the snow and the weather outside, it would be impossible to get my grandmother out of the house at all.

"Lord," I heard Grandpa pray softly, "right about now I could use one of your Christmas angels to come here and help me find a miracle." I fought back the tears as hard as I could, but they fell anyway. Silence is a heavy weight to bear when there doesn't seem to be a solution. And when I saw Grandpa Bill get worried, I got worried too. Just then the lights came back on and we all let out a sigh of relief.

Now, my dog Tinkerbell was busy lying on the red window chair, guarding the house as she always did, when all of a sudden she began to growl. Then she stood up and let out a loud snort and began to bark. Grandpa was clearly annoyed and got up to look out the window.

"What the heck is she barking about," he grumbled. Then all of a sudden, he called to Grandma. "Well, Cleo...I think I see someone walking down the road...a big fella with a military type hat but no gloves on. He looks like he just got out of the army."

He watched him trudging through the ever deepening snow and then said "You guys stay here, and I will go out to see what he needs." Then with a serious look on his face, he whispered low, "And Cleo...the gun is loaded and under the bed. Margie can grab it if you should need it. Understand?"

Grandma gave me a look, and my mouth must have been hanging wide open because the one rule in the house was I was never, ever to touch his gun. In my heart, I knew that this might not be a tired traveler, but maybe someone who could be a danger to us. Grandma couldn't shoot it, but I could—Grandpa had me practice all last summer. He said it was just in case there would be danger, and he couldn't be there to protect me, and that was all I needed to hear.

Grandpa got on his hat and coat and boots and went out into the storm, locking the door behind him. I got behind Grandma Cleo and pushed her wheelchair to where Tinker was. The three of us were silent and watched the two men talking. I saw Grandpa asking questions, and the man seemed to answer him okay enough, because all of a sudden I saw Grandpa put out his hand and the stranger took it. They shook hands and began to come toward the house. Grandma motioned for me to move her back into the kitchen. Then I went back into the living room and unlocked the door. I decided that I would go stand in Grandpa's room and wait to see if he would need his gun or not. I didn't want to lose the opportunity to be a help to my family if we needed it.

The door blew open with a huge gust of bitter wind and snow. The two men stomped their feet, shook off the snow from their shoulders, and walked toward the kitchen where Grandma was sitting. Tinker ran over to give him a nip at the ankle, but when she smelled him, she stopped and sat down. That amazed me, because she was known all over Colby's Point as the "little nipper." She nipped at everyone, friend or foe, who came into our house, so this behavior for her was really strange. I was sure that she would change her mind and attack, but she didn't. Tinkerbell was quiet and waited most patiently for the stranger to pay attention to her.

Grandpa composed himself and said, "This here is Dean Westergaurd. He is just out of the army, and his vehicle broke down all the way by Burton's bridge. With the snow and ice that was falling, he got all turned around here and was trying to find a filling station for help. I told him that I could take him over to the filling station once the storm dies down, but in the meantime, we didn't have much but he was welcome to what we had. If that is okay with you?"

Grandma turned her wheelchair toward the stranger and said, "Of course it is, Bill. Please have a seat, Mr. Westergaurd, and warm yourself for a bit. Although we won't be warm too much longer, it seems." Dean turned and smiled at me. He winked his eye, and suddenly I felt calm and safe with him in our house. Strange...I felt that I had known him somewhere else before.

"So is it your furnace that is broke? I see your lights getting dim. You know, my pa had his own furnace business when I was young, and if you want I could take a look at it for you," he offered. Between bites of Grandma's homemade meal, he went on to say, "While I was in the war, I also made sure that all the soldiers in my unit had the power that they needed.... There were some close calls out there."

For just a moment I saw my grandfather's eyes glaze over. After all, he'd been stationed over in France during the coldest months during World War II. The two men seemed to have that in common—the knowing of loss and the cold and the unending war.

Grandpa shook himself back to reality and said, "Seems fair enough, because I have to tell you—I was real worried about my wife and the girl here staying warm the next few days. Trying to get her into the car in her wheelchair...I didn't think I could do it by myself."

I noticed that as Grandpa talked, the big stranger was eating and drinking like it was the first food he had had all day. He also was looking around at the things in our kitchen. Fear and doubt crept in my mind for just a moment, but then Tinker came into the room and jumped right up in his lap and began to whimper.

"I have never seen her do that with anyone.... Tinker, get down!" Grandma swatted at her on his lap, but Dean just laughed and started to pet Tinkerbell. His laughter sounded like trumpets were being played. In fact, everyone in the room had great big smiles on their face. We all felt really good. It was almost like a family member had finally come home.

After Dean was done with his food, and he stood up and stretched. Then he said, "That was the best food I have had in a long time, Cleo. Now if you don't mind, you all stay in here, and I will be right back. I think I know how to fix this old, oil furnace for you."

I was smiling, but the smile suddenly turned to one of surprise. How did he know my grandma's name? I didn't recall Grandpa calling her by name. Just as I was about to ask, I felt a tugging on the back of my shirt. I swear, Grandma knew me like a book. She had caught it also but wanted me to keep my questions to myself.

Out he went, and after about ten minutes the lights came back on, and I heard the roar of the old furnace once again. My suspicions quickly dissipated. We all shouted hooray, and Grandma and Grandpa said they were going to offer him some more food to eat, and then Grandpa would drive him back to his car and help him get gas. We waited patiently for him to come back in from the cold backyard. I helped clear up the dishes and set out that plate of homemade cupcakes that Grandma had made earlier in the week. I suddenly remembered wondering why she had made more than usual, and felt that maybe this was something special for us on that cold night. Grandma always said there were no coincidences, only fate leading us gently by the hand.

Time was moving quickly now, and the soldier had not returned. Seeming somewhat impatient, Grandpa said, "Well, he should have come back in by now. I better go see what is going on out there." Grandpa got his coat and hat and gloves on and went out the same door as Dean had. After about ten minutes, I heard Grandpa coming through the garage door into the kitchen. I ran into the kitchen hoping to see the big friendly stranger one more time, but Grandpa came in alone. He walked right past me to the front door and went out and looked around and down the street. Coming back into the house, he sat down and just shook his head.

"Well, if that don't beat all. I can't find him! I looked at the furnace opening, and I looked all around the house, down the road, by the creek. I cannot find the young fellow anywhere. You know what the strangest thing of all is? There's only one set of footprints out there, and they're mine." Grandma wheeled into the room and listened as Grandpa tried to put some reason to it. He pointed out that this big, tall stranger named Dean Westergaurd had come into our home, ate soup, drank coffee, and was going to come in for some of Grandma's wonderful cupcakes after he fixed our furnace...and then he disappeared.

Getting up some nerve, I said, "Maybe God answered your prayers, Grandpa, and sent an angel to come here and fix our furnace."

Grandma and Grandpa didn't argue, but Grandpa got on the phone. Before I knew it, Sheriff Fino was on his way to our house. He listened as he took down the story from all of us talking at once and then sat down for cupcakes and coffee. He promised to have some information for us on this stranger as soon as he could. As he left, he double-checked our house to make sure we were safe.

A few days went by, and the experience was still so strong with all of us that we all seemed to be lost in our own thoughts of reasoning. I remembered the story that Grandma Cleo had told me about the angel who had helped the town in trouble, and I thought that maybe my talking aloud during my walk might have brought the help that we needed.

Finally, Sheriff Fino came back to see us. He walked in and went into the kitchen with a report of some kind in his hands. "Bill, Cleo... Now, I have known you to be good people. You live by God's Word, and I know that neither of you abuse the drink, but what I have to tell you is as strange as the story is that you told me." I stood holding my breath to see if this was a miracle after all. "All I can say is, sometimes things happen and we have to step back and accept that the good Lord always watches over us." Sheriff Fino cleared his throat and shuffled his papers. "This report states that the Dean Westergaurd you told me about was a specialist in the army during World War II where he was killed. He was a family man, from Richmond, Illinois. He was a hero, decorated for saving half his platoon, and his specialty in the war was working the portable furnaces that kept our soldiers warm while in combat. His son and granddaughter still live in Richmond today. Here is a picture of Dean Westergaurd."

The sheriff handed the picture over to Grandpa, who passed it to Grandma. I peered over her shoulder. That was him! That was the gentle stranger who had come to our house for help and ended up helping us.

The sheriff continued. "His son says that they have had other calls and reports from other counties of a Dean Westergaurd helping people in need when their homes get cold. They said that you could keep this picture of him, and they only ask a few favors of you, in all of this."

"What's that?" I chirped out loud.

The sheriff stood there for a minute, and I saw that there were tears in his eyes. Then he said, "They want you all to share his story to those who are hurting. And if you come across someone in need, you make sure that they are not cold or hungry or lost. And they hope you always and forever keep this miracle in your heart."

We all nodded our heads in agreement to never forget that a Christmas angel came to our home and helped us stay warm. That evening as we all sat together looking at the Christmas tree in our front room and listening to some Christmas carols on the radio, it came to me that the true miracle of Christmas is when we love unconditionally and never, ever expect a return back to us for a good deed that we do with our heart. Watch your fellow man and be kind, because someday you may need a miracle, or someday you may be a miracle to someone else. There are times that we may have the opportunity to sit with angels.

I sat holding my dog Tinkerbell as I looked outside at the stars, and all I knew was that an angel had made a difference to me and my grandparents, and Christmas was never going to be the same.

May the peace of the season bring you the opportunity to be that miracle to someone in need, and may the angels that are around you comfort you and hold your hands in your time of need.

Chapter Four

THE CHRISTMAS DEER

Grandpa had a way with every living thing. It seemed that every living creature at some time or another came here to us, to him. With his gentle heart and strong hands, even the most timid of animals trusted him...

To wound a deer in leap so high
Is haunting I've heard tell
Tis but the story of his death
And then the forest's still...

*I*t was almost Christmas again in our whimsical little pink house in Colby Point. It was 1960 and I was six years old. Living near the beautiful green banks of the Fox River provided endless opportunities and experiences. One of the most magical things about this place was how the wild animals of the area all seemed to trust my grandpa. They ventured into our yard at various times in search of food or help or sometimes just curious on what breed of animal lived in a pink box. I had to be really careful when I went into the woods, because hunters would drift close to our land.

One day, I was in the backyard working feverishly to find the hidden acorns that had fallen to the ground and now were covered with the first layer of snow. I needed enough acorns to fill the pretty glass jar that I had, so I could tie a red ribbon around it and give it to my grandma for Christmas. I was also finding pinecones that had fallen from our trees and red berries from the holly bush that grew across the street in my aunts' front yard. Everywhere I looked, there was a treasure to be found.

All of a sudden, there was a gunshot. Tinkerbell yelped as she ran frantically into the garage, and Grandpa called for me to come into the house. I ran home as fast as I could, leaving all my gathered acorns scattered across the snow. Once I was safe inside, Grandma and I looked out the back window as Grandpa spotted a young buck stumbling across the cornfield into our backyard.

Grandpa ran back into the house and told us, "That young buck, he's shot. Cleo, where's the vegetables that ya cut up for dinner? I need them now!"

Grandma wheeled herself into the kitchen and pulled open the icebox. There in her best yellow bowl were our dinner vegetables that were going to be put in her roast that night. Grandpa proceeded to strip down to just his shorts. Then he took all the apples, carrots, and potatoes and sliced them all in half to get at their juice. Then my grandfather did the strangest thing: he rubbed all those vegetables all over his body—hands, arms, chest and legs. Then he took a fresh handkerchief that Grandma had just pressed and dipped it in the vegetable water to hide his scent on that. Then he walked out into the cold and right up to the young deer. The buck was in shock, so he didn't run or even blink. Grandpa touched him and made a cooing sound in the back of his throat to soothe the deer. Then he covered the deer's eyes with the handkerchief and led him right into our garage.

Grandpa must have been out there for thirty minutes before he finally came back in. When he did, he was shivering so badly that his false teeth just about came loose from his mouth. Grandma was fit to be tied.

"What's wrong with you, Bill Mauer? Don't you know you will catch your death of cold? No one has been able to help a deer that's been shot in the wild; why are you doing this? You should just put the poor thing out of his misery."

Grandpa took a deep breath and whispered, "Listen, he was just grazed across his chest. It didn't even break the muscle—just scraped him—and he is in shock. He'll be all right; he just needs a few days of quiet and warmth and food. So let's try this, and I promise that if it don't work, I'll put him down. In the meantime, I need both of you to keep your voices down and walk quietly in the house." He turned and pointed at my toy fox terrier pup. "And that goes for you too, Tinkerbell," he said.

So for the next three days—and believe me, these were the longest three days of my life—Tinkerbell and I played as quietly as possible. I read more books than usual and painted with Grandma in the afternoons. At night instead of television, Grandpa told us about growing up in the wilderness of Marshfield, Wisconsin, and the people that he knew and the Native American Indians who had lived nearby. It was really a wonderful time that we spent in those three days because, just like in olden days, there would be a kind of resurrection of a beautiful being that was wounded by man and saved by another man's kindness and faith. Grandpa had the kind of faith that could move mountains. If he believed in it, it would be. That was the plain and simple rule that he lived by. I was able to learn so much about who I was at that time in my life.

A gentle and steady rush of tears would pop every now and again, and Grandma said it was my soul connecting to that of the deer in our garage. I knew she was right, and was honored to be a part of this rescue. I wondered how long it would be before the deer was ready to be set free. Soon it was the third morning. Suddenly, maybe around five in the morning, a loud banging started from the garage. It was the deer, and he wanted out. Grandpa jumped from his bed and ran into the garage.

Grandma was still in bed, so she yelled at me, "I can't watch, but look out the front window and see if you can see the deer running free. Oh, I wish I was up!"

Tinkerbell and I sat motionless at the window, and all of a sudden the garage door flew up, and the young buck ran out of the garage and stopped in our front yard as if to get his bearing. He sniffed the air, looked around, and licked his wound. Turning, he looked eye-to-eye with Grandpa and then, in a split second, he was gone. He bounded across our lawn and past Aunt Malita's house. I shouted out the details to Grandma.

When Grandpa came in to the house, he got Grandma out of bed and we got settled in for breakfast. Our prayer that morning was one of thankfulness because our Lord worked through Grandpa's hands so that this deer could be saved and live on.

Life settled down and seasons changed. Spring burst into this small world of mine, and the wildflowers that came from the April rain kept me busy right through the dog days of summer and into the warm and enticing waves of the Fox River. I kept hoping that maybe I would see the deer that Grandpa saved, but I never did. Soon fall came and went in a flurry of different colors, and before long it was Christmas once again. It could be lonely at the end of the road, but there always seemed to be magic in the air out there.

Grandma was up early, cutting up the vegetables for our Christmas dinner that she would make later that day. I was in a deep sleep, dreaming that I was fishing and that a fish was pulling on my big toe. I woke up to find Grandpa doing just that.

"Hey, Margie, wake up! I have something to show ya. Get up real quiet and come out into the livin' room and look out the front window. Your grandma's waitin' for ya."

Rubbing my eyes, I slowly crawled out of bed, grabbed my blanket, and walked up to the big red chair that backed up to our front window. Grandma was already there, and Tinkerbell was standing on the top of the chair in her favorite place, but she was shivering with excitement. Grandpa was undressed to his shorts, and

Grandma was muttering under her breath that he was going to catch his death from the cold.

I looked out at the small slope that joined our property with Aunt Malita's. There stood a huge buck, his doe, and two small fawns. They were all nosing around the grass looking for morsels to eat. I heard our door open and shut softly, and I saw Grandpa going toward them with an apple in his hands. Then he stopped and stood real still. The doe and her young fawns were startled and ran to the edge of the lawn, where they stopped and turned and watched as the buck came toward Grandpa, bowing his head and allowing Grandpa to run his hand over the scar on his chest, left from the bullet wound he had received the Christmas before.

This was Grandpa's deer! He'd come back to show Grandpa that he was okay and that because of Grandpa's kindness, he'd had the chance to live on and have a family of his own.

The buck bent his head way down, and Grandpa reached up. A piece of the antler covering came off in his hands. It was a gift from the buck to Grandpa, a giving-back of thankfulness. They stood close together—I imagine only for a minute or two, but it sure seemed to go on for hours. Time stood still as we, just the humans of the house, witnessed a bonding of two beings that walked along this earth with beautiful souls. The buck moved back, and his family anxiously started to move down the yard and into the forest. Grandpa came back in, all excited.

"Did you see that, Cleo? Did you? That was my deer! He made it and...and...*achoo!*"

Grandma moved her wheelchair toward Grandpa, all the time scolding him. "What did I tell you...being a fool out there in your skivvies?! Get in the kitchen and have some of that Jack Daniels that you have been saving for something special."

My grandparents were busy recounting the events of that morning. Tinkerbell began to bark right along with their talking, just to add her two cents. Me, I could not move and I promised myself that I would never forget the time I saw the magical moment between Grandpa and his Christmas deer.

Life was always teaching me things, giving me opportunities to learn and to be the witness of its miracles. Sometimes it was a simple rose that Grandpa would cut and give to Grandma in the small jelly glass, and sometimes it was something so big that only the entire world that I lived in could be the place for it to all happen. When I think of this time, I feel its faith and hope and love. Grandpa had a love for all things, animal and human alike. It didn't matter to him who or what you were—we were supposed to love all beings that walked on God's earth.

I can still hear him now, saying, "Out of all God's graces, these three things remain: faith, hope, and love. But remember, Margie, that the greatest of these is love."

Chapter Five

THE RED RIBBON

She could not stop and wait for death
As close as it could seem
The driver watched and held his breath
For all eternity
Red Ribbons fell from clouds above
On trees with branches bare
As if to color all its limbs
And say that she did care
We are our brother's keeper,
Our love should never cease
A simple gesture just from you
Of brotherhood and peace....

❦

*I*t was November 23, 1961, and I was seven-and-three-quarters-years old, soon to be eight. Well, in February anyway, which wasn't too far away. Grandma Cleo and Grandpa Bill had hosted a wonderful Thanksgiving dinner the day before with all the traditional goodies. My mother and soon-to-be stepfather Marty came out, and it was great to have the small house busy with the sounds of good conversation and laughter. Even though it was all cleaned up and put away now, there was a lingering scent of fullness. Sweet potatoes, stuffing, and the turkey were all wrapped up, waiting for Grandpa to sneak in and grab some more!

Tradition hung heavily in the little pink house at the end of Colby Point Road. Once Thanksgiving was over, it was clean-up time, and everyone knew that Grandma Cleo wanted the work to be done so we could enjoy the next holiday—Christmas!

Christmas was never rushed, not in this house. The first thing Grandma did was give us each our Christmas list of things to do. Then she would get her Christmas cards ready to send out to family, friends, and neighbors. Then there was the cooking...oh, the Christmas cookies she could bake! My favorite was the sugar cut-out cookies that she would painstakingly paint with her secret frosting. I loved to take a Santa cookie and admire the red frosting for his coat and pants, his white beard, and chocolate-flavored boots. I loved them so much that every time I got one, I would bite its head off!

Grandpa's list consisted of cleaning out the front room so that the tree would have room to breathe. Then he would have to go up to the attic and get down the beloved ornaments that Grandma Cleo had collected all through the years. Do you know that I have saved her spinning star ornaments? It has been years since she hung them on our tree, but every year since then, they have been on mine. One faded red and two pale blue ornaments, each with a small, spinning, silver star in the middle. They held such magic for me as a child, and even though I am an adult now, my heart thrills every time I see them start to spin again.

My list was the best one in the house. I got to go outside and gather acorns, pinecones, red berries, and holly to help decorate the tree. I got to fill up the bird and squirrel feeders so that our yard was full of life. And the last thing I got to do at Christmas was go door to door to the homes of the neighbors who had decided to tough it out and stay here in Colby Point for the winter. We would give them a card with a red ribbon in it along with some cookies from Grandma. The cookies were for eating, and the ribbon was to go around something in their front yard to celebrate the true meaning of Christmas. Grandma said that the true meaning of Christmas was that we as people were all bound together with brotherhood and peace.

In years past, Grandpa had pulled out my red wooden sled and stacked all the goodies on it, along with me and my dog Tinker. Then Grandpa pulled the sled along the snow-covered dirt road, and I ran and dropped off the packages at each house. But this year was going to be different because I was almost eight, and Grandpa said it was time that I could do it myself. Grandma didn't care for that idea, but I promised not to go past the fork in the road, and I'd have Tinker with me so I was perfectly safe.

"Please, please, please!" I begged until Grandma relented.

"Oh, all right. But you know the rules—only to the homes where someone is there, and not past the fork in the road." She turned her head and looked at Tinker who sat really still, waiting for her orders. "That goes for you, too, Tinkerbell," she added sternly. "I am holding you responsible!" Tinker yelped and spun around and around in circles as I got busy getting all my winter clothes on.

There were twelve homes on our little dirt road up to the fork. But only seven of those homes, not including ours, were occupied in the winter months. It's funny how a small thing like a fork in the road can define who you know and who you don't. Oh don't get me wrong—my grandparents knew everyone on our street from beginning to end and then around again toward the creek. We were well known, too! Ours was a house of love, laughter, and magic. Most of the folks in the area came to my grandpa when there was trouble of some sort. I always looked at him as kind of a sheriff, the sheriff of Colby Point.

There were more houses past the fork in the road, and I was very curious about the people who lived in them—and one person in particular. Her name was Penelope Nickel, or Penny Nickel for short. Aunt Sylvia told us stories about her when my cousins visited. We would be taking a walk around the circle, beginning at the end of our dirt road, through the woods, over the creek, past the haunted mink farm, and finally over the small hill where the fork in the road was. Aunt Sylvia would always talk in hushed tones as she told the older relatives of Penny's strange ways and hardship. My aunt wasn't always kind, but she held sympathies in her heart for Penny.

To go left toward our house was the safe and right way to go, but to go right toward the other end of the road meant you would pass the homes of the unusual folks who came and went like the seasons each year. Penny Nickels was a spinster who was born and raised in the house she lived in. Her folks had both died there, as did her brother and best dog. She had pinkish hair, wore too much blush (at least that's what we were told), and her windows and doors were covered so no light got in and none of her got out. Aunt Sylvia said that she'd seen Penny one time in town years ago, but when she'd tried to talk to her, Penny hissed at Aunt Sylvia, then ran to her old car and drove off.

I decided to ask my grandma about Penny and why we didn't give her cookies and a red ribbon each year.

"Grandma, can I ask you something?"

"Seems to me you're going to anyway, I'm a-thinkin', so get on with it." She was finishing a painting of a beautiful lady dancing with a scruffy-looking man.

"I want to give Penny Nickels some cookies and a red ribbon this year." There, I'd said it! I held my breath, waiting for Grandma to reprimand me for telling her who to give cookies to this year. But instead she was quiet and then put her brush down and looked at me real close.

"Let me tell you something that maybe no one ever told you before," she said. "When you were just a baby and you were here with us all alone, Penny used to come and clean up the house. She needed some extra money, and we needed the help. I knew her mother and father real well and Penny, well, she was a different kind of a loner and a low talker if you know what I mean?"

I didn't but I shook my head yes anyway, wanting her to continue.

"One day close to the holidays, Penny came on Thursday afternoon at 1:23—the same time every week for a year. Grandpa was at the store, and you were taking a nap with Tinker. We got to talking—or tryin' to—and I asked her why she wanted to be alone like she was and not married with family. I guess I was just curious and pushed too hard asking her questions and all."

Grandma paused again and let out a sign that seemed to go on forever. Then she said, "Penny stopped what she was doing and said to me, 'There's no one for me, no one to care.... I prefer not to care back. That way, I never hurt.'" Grandma shifted her weight in her chair and continued on with her story, "There was a silence that hung in the air like a humid night. It got real warm in our house and still; so still that I swear I could hear her thoughts. Penny blinked, and I saw the start of a tear in her eye. I never got to reply 'cause Penny walked out and never came back. I tried that year to leave her cookies and a ribbon, but they ended up back at our house on the step the following morning. Leave things alone, child. Some people are happiest in their misery."

That night as I was in bed and saying my prayers, I asked God to bless Penny Nickels, and I asked him to forgive me because I was going to break one of Grandma's rules. I was going past the fork in the road.

The next morning was Christmas Eve, and the house was busy. Grandpa had the living room ready, and we were going for our tree. It was a short walk through the cornfield behind our house into the valley where Grandpa planted Christmas trees each year to replenish what we took. We chose a beautiful tree, very full, and all glittery in the sunlight because of the ice that was on it from the night before. It smelled of wood and pine from my valley. I called it mine because no one ever came to that valley except me and Grandpa and Tinker. It was my place to be, to talk to God, and to let my secret thoughts out. Every tree was covered in snow with bluish icicles hanging off their limbs. It was a winter wonderland indeed.

Tinker barked all the way there and all the way home. When we got back, Grandma had everything ready to go and also had some hot chocolate in my thermos, so when I was out delivering the cookies I'd have something warm to drink. She gave me a huge bag of red ribbons that I was supposed to tie onto the trees along the way. Grandma told me not to lose them as she would have Grandpa tie the extras up on our trees outside so that anyone who came this way would know that this was a home of brotherhood and peace.

"There'll be plenty left, Margie, so when you bring them back, leave them on the swing on the front of the house," Grandma instructed. When she wasn't looking, I reached up and grabbed an extra box of cookies and a Christmas card that I slipped under my scarf and hat.

Calling Tinker, I told my grandparents I would be home after delivering the cookies and wishing our neighbors a Merry Christmas from all of us. The first two homes on the left of the street belonged to my three aunts and to Alfred and Greta Boldt. Those houses were empty, as they all went somewhere warm for the winter. The third house was Carrie and Irv Medlinger's house, and it was decorated and ready for visitors.

Carrie greeted me with lots of laughter as she caught me in her arms for a bear hug. Irv took the cookies and card and ran and got the gift that they had for me, along with some fudge for Grandma and Grandpa. I loved their home—it was warm and all the walls and ceilings were done in hardwood. I always felt as if I were in a log cabin when I went there. Carrie was a large, strong woman whom I had come to trust when she helped my grandmother one day after a fall. It was good to know I had friends that I could trust on our little street.

On I went, house by house, until I was done. My sled was loaded with gifts and foods and even some homemade honey from the Fergusons' fall harvest from their own beehive. I turned around and looked toward my house. I could see a glimmer of light in the window, as it was starting to get dark. Tinker was on the sled wrapped up in a small blanket and started to whine at me. But I had my mind set. I told Tinker to just hang on a darn minute as I got up the courage to make my feet move past the fork in the road.

Finally, after what seemed like forever, I walked past Theresa Bach's house and Tootsie's house and on around the bend. It seemed darker and much more still on this end of the road. Turning around...my house was gone, and it kept getting farther away as I walked down the road. I saw a light coming from a grayish looking house that had neither driveway nor sidewalk going up to it. The mailbox was bent and rusted almost all the way through. But the name was clear—P. NICKELS. I had made it there, and somehow I found the courage to walk all the way to the small home nestled in the snow near the riverbank.

I saw a light leaking out of a side window and heard noises coming from inside. Tinker growled at me, and I knew she wanted me to go home...but I had come so far. I had to do this. I walked toward the door with the box of cookies and card in my hands, but as I went to knock on her door, it opened up. There she stood, maybe a few inches taller than me, red-colored cheeks and lips and, yes, her hair was pinkish...kind of. I couldn't talk. I just held the box of cookies and the card out to her.

She stared at me and said, "You're Margie, Cleo's grandbaby, all grown up. I never thought I'd see you again," she said. She leaned around me and looked at what I had on my sled. "Grab Tinker and get in here before you freeze to death." I was shocked that she knew my dog's name, but I did as I was told. Once inside I took a good look around so as not to forget what I was being allowed to see. I suddenly realized that every single lamp was lit. There must have been a hundred lamps, or so it seemed. The lamps gave off so much heat that I started to take off my hat and gloves and unwrap Tinkerbell.

"How'd you know my dog's name was Tinker?" was all that I could get out.

"I was the one who told your grandparents on where to get her. I had her brother Tiger, but he got sick and died a few years back." She pointed to a dusty frame, and in it was a picture of my dog Tinker and her brother Tiger as pups. I also saw one of my grandmother's paintings on her wall. It was if she could read my mind. Grandma didn't give her pictures away easily, and I knew that Penny had to have meant something to Grandma for her to give her such a beautiful painting.

"Yes, child, that painting is one your grandma did for me. It is of the ocean, as she knew I would never see one." Walking toward the painting, she touched it and whispered low, "Your grandma must be the kindest person that I have ever met." As I listened, I knew I should go home, but I was so curious about what my grandmother had told me about her that I came right out and asked her.

"Why did you go away and never come back to our house? Why did you stop being by everybody?" It took forever for her to answer. Penny walked around the room, holding onto the furniture for support. She seemed to be lost in her thoughts. She stood and stared at a picture of a family on the wall for a long time. Then she turned around and walked back toward me and stood really close to my face.

"I guess I lost the spirit," Penny said. "That warm feeling you get when you hear a family member's voice, or you smell something that brings back that feeling of belonging.... But you wouldn't understand, and I don't feel like explaining anymore to you or anyone else! I think it's time for you to go now. I know your grandma and grandpa wouldn't like you being out in the dark and away from them this long." She started to push me toward the door. On the way, I noticed that she had quite a few empty boxes of hot chocolate mix stacked up on the floor.

"My...my grandma Cleo makes the best hot chocolate in the whole world!" I blurted out.

As Penny pushed me out the door, I heard her say, "I remember," and that was it. She was gone, and I was outside all sweaty and teary-eyed.

I didn't even care that I was going to be in trouble for being gone so long. I cared more that she was alone. I stood on my tiptoes and looked under the board that kept the light in. I could see her walking toward the back of her house. The room was misty looking like the fog had crept in from the river, but that can't happen in winter, only in fall when the warm water hits the cool air. She stumbled and then held onto a chair...and then walked right out of the house—only not through the back door but like a ghost right through the wall or so I thought. With the light so bright and the shadows on the walls it seemed to give an illusion that she was a ghost!

I could not believe my eyes, and I held my breath as Tinker began to howl, which was something she never did. I was scared to death. I grabbed my sled and ran toward home as fast as I could.

Somewhere along the way, I must have dropped the bag of extra red ribbons that Grandma had told me to be sure to bring home for Grandpa to use. Tinker was ahead of me, and I could hear Grandpa using my Oscar Mayer whistle, letting me know that it was time to come home.

I was never as glad as I was that night to be home with the ones who loved me and all the wonderful things we had. I had a home and food and a dog and family. I had so much more than Penny Nickels, and the thought of her being alone gave me such a sad feeling. In fact, I was so sad that I didn't care that it was Christmas Eve. That night when I was going to bed, Grandma called me to her bedside. She told me to come up close to her, and she looked at me really long. I wanted to tell her what I did, but I was scared and sad and ashamed because I had never told her a lie before...not ever. Grandma patted the empty side of her bed for me to sit down. I was flushed and fighting the tears. For a little while, Grandma simply looked at me, and then I had had enough. I lay down next to her and could feel her breathing in and out. I could feel her thoughts and her love for me.

"It's okay, Margie. I think in the morning things will be clearer, and then we can talk. After all, Santa comes tonight, and you had Grandpa tie the red ribbons on the trees outside so that Santa saw that we were being good and following his rules of brotherhood and peace, right?"

I couldn't answer; I just nodded my head yes. And you know, I think she knew all along what I had done. But she simply let me go to bed and stew in it all night. And it was a very long night indeed. I could hear Grandpa in the bed near me snoring lightly as the night grew darker. I could hear the night train in the distance, and I wanted so badly to be able to run far away...far enough away so that the hurt that Penny Nickels talked about wouldn't grow inside of me.

I finally fell asleep and had dreams of Penny's house with no boards on the windows. A house with a sidewalk that went to her front door and of a family in her home, laughing and sharing the warmth that only family could share. I dreamt that she was young with children of her own and that even her little dog was alive and well. As I turned to go home, I could hear her calling me back... over and over. I continued to hear my name being called until I recognized it as the voice of Grandma Cleo. Getting up, I reached for Tinker, but she was already gone. I stretched and looked outside, and it had snowed. In our backyard, a family of deer was busy licking the salt block that I had placed on the wood for them. The squirrels were scrambling to get their nuts, and I swear that every colored bird that God created was busy eating in our bird feeders! I walked into the kitchen, and there at my spot was my breakfast and a beautiful Christmas cookie that Grandma had made just for me. Grandma and Grandpa were sitting there waiting for me, just sipping on their coffee.

Usually I couldn't eat breakfast because the anticipation of the gifts that were waiting for me was too much to bear, but this Christmas morning I looked at my grandparents, and I think I really saw them for the first time. Grandpa was tall and thin and brown colored, even in the winter, since he spent most of his days outside working in the garden and fixing our home and taking care of living things...human and creature. When he smiled, he had lines that connected all over his face. His eyes twinkled with mischief, and his voice always had a matching chuckle in it. His hair was white and soft and thick. His hands showed the years of hard work and love. Strong and calloused yet gentle to touch and be touched.

Grandma—well, she was peace. She was calm, and she was everything that I wanted to be. Maybe she couldn't walk, but there was nowhere that she hadn't been in her life walking or traveling in spirit. I felt a funny warmth come over me, and then Grandpa's voice brought me back to the moment.

"What's got into you, girl? Why aren't ya tearing up the gifts under the tree that Santa left ya last night?" Not to make him suspicious, I didn't say a word but went into the front room with Tinker at my side and looked at the gifts under the tree.

I heard Grandma say, "She's growing up, Bill. She's becoming aware of that brotherhood we have talked about to her since she was young." I remembered the red ribbons, and my heart sank because I realized that I had let my grandparents down by losing them as I ran home from Penny Nickel's house. I walked back into the kitchen and started to tell them what I had done. I told them everything—the people I saw on Colby Point Road and finally my visit to Penny Nickel's house. I confessed that I'd lost the red ribbons, and I cried such tears that I just couldn't talk anymore. I cried because I wanted to make the pain go away for Penny, and I didn't know how to do it.

Grandpa stood up and scratched his head the way he did when he was puzzled about something. Then he said, "But the red ribbons were on our trees when I got up this morning. I thought that you did it last evening before coming in. I was going to tell you that I would rather you not use my ladder to place them so high on the top of the trees, 'cause you could have fallen...."

Grandpa and I both saw the look on Grandma's face as she turned her head quickly to hide the tears. Grandpa and I went to the big picture window, and every tree in our yard, all the way up to the top, had the red ribbons on them. We looked at them and at each other more than once. Finally we walked back into the kitchen where Grandma sat quietly with her eyes closed.

After a few moments she composed herself and said, "Sit down, both of you, because I have something to tell you." We sat down at the table. "While you were sleeping, Margie, and while Grandpa had Tinker outside, the phone rang. It seems that Sheriff Fino was called by a neighbor from beyond the fork in the road. They had heard some commotion out by Penny Nickel's place, and they were concerned that someone may have broken into her home."

A sick feeling started to grow in my stomach, and I hoped that the neighbor didn't blame me for the intrusion at Penny's home.

"When the sheriff got to her home, he knocked and knocked, and there was no answer. He went inside, and every single lamp was on in her home, but Penny was nowhere to be found.... until he went out to the backyard, that is. That's where he found her. She must have been sick and passed away in the snow. The sheriff said that there was no sign of foul play, but he wanted us to have our cookies back.... I gave the cookies to him, as he does good work."

Grandma wheeled her chair toward the front window and began to look at the trees outside, all covered in red ribbons. "He said that there was a smaller set of footprints that he followed all the way to our house. He said that when he got here, he had never seen so many red ribbons before in the trees. He didn't ask me about the footprints but just kept commenting on the red ribbons on the trees in our yard. So it got me to thinkin'…. If you didn't do it, Bill, and Margie didn't either, then I think that Penny may have paid us a visit and gave us a gift that she could never give to anyone else—the love of brotherhood and peace."

We all fell silent, lost in our own thoughts. It seemed that the miracles we always talked about had surprised us and given us a miracle of our own that year. That Christmas stayed with us a bit longer than usual…we left those ribbons up on the trees permanently. Years drifted by and my grandparents both passed away and I ended up selling their house to a nice older couple looking for a safe and quiet place to retire.

I wanted to see it once more in the snow, so this past Christmas, my husband and I took a ride out there through the woods, over the river, and down that little dirt road. As we pulled up in front of the little pink house, I looked at the once small trees that have now grown taller than the house. At the tips of the trees, there were still pieces of those red ribbons. They've faded with time and the weather, but each one stayed strong in all its glory.

Penny Nichols may have been lonely in her life here on earth, but in the afterworld she found the love that she had lost. I remember that night so well—the feeling of loneliness that Penny shared with me, but also the lesson of love and what this time of year stands for.

Hope…brotherhood and peace.

Chapter Six

Minerva the Mermaid

I wonder what did swim beneath the creek not straight but round
The treasures that were given were the worms beneath the ground
As I stood and held my breath the tail was long and sleek
The air was warm, the sun so bright I hoped to get a peek
Now legend says that sisters two were witches in the wood
Two sisters there were all alone they held their hands and stood
But one day long ago it's told a fight between them fell
One remained a human being and one we cannot tell
Her fate was not an easy one where legs a tail grew
Her body once an hour glass was something scaled and new
A smaller head with hair so straight instead of hair that curled
And when she dove beneath the pond the water swirled and swirled
This mystery seems perplexing and some will not think true
But I know she still swims beneath the water round and blue.

ᔆ

*I*t was the summer of my eighth year which was in 1962. School was out, friends were vacationing back to Colby Point but still I was bored. There were trees to climb, rabbits and squirrels to watch, and even a lazy creek at my toes that flowed into the fast-running Fox River, but I was bored and that always meant trouble. Sunday was always the day that dragged the most. The aunts across the street already had their day planned. After church, they always went into town for some bakery sweets. Aunts Dula, Lily, and Sylvia also took Aunt Malita with them, because she had to have her peppermints.

Grandma and Grandpa had just about had enough of my endless chatter when they pushed me and my dog Tinkerbell out the door.

"Go on out, Margie, and see if Peggy can come out to play," said Grandma Cleo.

"But we had a fight, and I don't want to be the first one to start talkin'." I muttered it under my breath because Grandma didn't like back talk. Still grumbling, I headed out with Tinker close behind me.

The path was just about worn down from my house to Peggy's. I walked down the dried-up grass to the dirt path that led into the green forest and to the slow-moving creek and the small makeshift wooden bridge that crossed it. Standing on the bridge, I watched Tinker nose around underneath trying to catch a minnow or two. I was always amazed at how slow this part of the creek was and how fast other parts were. Grandpa said that this was a cursed creek because the flow didn't run right. Water always runs down toward a main source, but this part of the creek had been dammed up by old man Grier.

Mr. Grier wanted Grandpa to sell him some riverfront land that he owned, but Grandpa wouldn't do it because Mr. Grier wanted to build it all up. So Mr. Grier cut off the flow to our part of the creek. At one time, all Grandpa had to do was throw his line in, and he could catch huge catfish like nothing. Once Mr. Grier dammed the creek, though, the water would flow down to a certain point, and then it would turn around and come back up. It was really weird. It was like it was all confused. But because this creek didn't flow as fast as the other parts, I felt very safe wading in its cool waters.

But even that can be boring, so I put my stubborn pride aside and walked slowly to Peggy Walker's house. I looked around for Tinker, hoping she'd give me some support, but she was stretched out on the ground with her legs in the air, rubbing her back in the dirt. She wiggled and wriggled and paid no attention to me and my problems. I held my breath and knocked on the door. I heard some muffled voices, and finally Peggy opened the door. The sun was shining in her eyes so she was squinting one eye shut, chewing on gum so hard that I could see that she had lost another tooth. I thought I saw her smile slightly at being the victor in our latest tussle.

We stood there for what seemed like an eternity, when all of a sudden, someone from behind her gave her a shove and yelled, "So what are ya waiting for? Are you gonna talk or are the two of you just gonna stare at each other?" It was her older brother, Robert. He always gave us a hard time when we hung out at Peggy's house.

Peggy pushed back. Having four older brothers made her a tough little girl. Her mother wasn't well and her father was gone a lot...and when he was home, everyone stayed out of his way. The more I thought about it, the more I realized just how lucky I was to have my grandparents raising me.

Finally, I blurted out, "I wanted to come over and tell you that I forgive you, and I know that you can be crabby sometimes, and even though I was right, well, maybe... Do ya want to hang out and go skipping stones or something?"

She looked at me for a minute and replied, "Are you batty or something? You forgive me? I have better things to do than hang around with you. Why don't you go down and visit the Myatts and see what Sylvee has in her pocket? And by the way...I don't forgive you!"

And with that, Peggy slammed the door in my face. I was surprised at the suddenness of her actions and almost fell off that front step. Tinker was long gone and home again, and I was standing there with egg on my face while Peggy and her stupid brothers whooped it up behind their battered and stained front door.

I stood there for a minute mustering my reply. I would show her! As loud as I could, I shouted, "Oh yeah? Well that sounds like a grand idea to me, Miss Peggy Walker! I don't care if my grandpa said I was never to go to Sylvee Myatt's house by myself, I am going anyway!"

And off I strutted up the gravel road, past the huge cabin cruiser boat that the Adimites kept in their front yard, past Paul Demarco's wild horses, and around the turn to the ugliest, dirtiest, scariest house there was in all of Colby Point. I was so mad that, before I could stop myself, I was knocking on the door. I must have stopped somewhere between knocks number three and four when the door opened up slowly. It was Ma Myatt, who was not much taller than I was. It was rumored that she was a little person, even though most people used slang words that Grandma Cleo told me weren't the Christian thing to say.

I lost my breath sort of, and I must have looked scared because Ma Myatt smiled a big, toothless smile at me.

"You here for Sylvee?"

"Um, yes. I am. Can she come out to play?"

Ma Myatt looked me up and down and said, real close to my face, "Are ya that Mauer girl from the other side? Do your folks know y'are here? ... Never mind, I'll get her for ya." As she turned to get Sylvee, I saw the other sister, Irene. She was a Down syndrome girl and very big for her age. She just stood and stared at me. I was so uncomfortable that I started to giggle, and that made her giggle too. There were nine Myatt children in the house, seven brothers and two sisters. I remember hearing Aunt Malita talking to Grandma Cleo in hushed tones about their "situation" and how they didn't belong here in Colby Point—that their kind always brought trouble with them and that their kids had no manners or dignified upbringing. Grandma shamed Aunt Malita and said that most people that moved here had situations, and no one was better than the other. I always wondered if the word "situation" was a bad label to have but was glad that I didn't have it! When Sylvee came to the door, she gave me a big hug. Sylvee always had a smile on her face. She didn't have the best of clothes, nor were they clean. Not too many kids were nice to her because their family was poor, but that never stopped her from being friendly and nice...and sometimes a bit scary!

"Hey there, Margie," she greeted me. "You want to come with me to feed Minerva? Look what I have for her in my pocket."

Before I even knew what Sylvee was talking about, she reached into her pocket and pulled out a huge handful of dirt. I put my face closer and to my surprise I saw a huge earthworm wiggling around in the dirt. I jumped back with a start and that made Sylvee laugh and then Irene started in laughing to.

"What are you gonna do with that?" I asked the already dirt-stained Sylvee.

Irene snorted in the background, saying "Minerva" really long and low, breaking up the syllables—"Maa-nerr-veaa!"

She kept saying it over and over and faster and faster until Sylvee turned around and told her to *be quiet!* Irene seemed not to care and just kept saying the name over and over but a bit quieter now.

"I am going down to the circle creek to feed Minerva. She is beautiful and waits for me every morning to come and bring her breakfast." Sylvee held that fat wiggly worm up in the air and pretended to eat it.

"Stop it, Sylvee!" I backed up a little. "Who or what is a Minerva?"

Sylvee just smiled at me and grabbed my hand. Next thing I knew, we were off to the circle creek.

Now, I knew I was already in trouble because I had gone farther than the boundaries of Peggy's house. I could hear Grandpa's whistle, letting me know that I had been gone too long. But I didn't care and really wanted to see this Minerva creature that she was talking about, so I ignored my better sense and went down the road toward the creek that I had only heard about from others.

The legend of the circle creek was that it had belonged to a witch named Fena. She had lived there, it was told, for almost one hundred years until someone found her dead in the garden, being eaten by wild things from the forest. Grandpa's sisters—my aunts across the street—would take family members that were out for a visit for the long fateful walk to the old broken-down "glass house" that she'd lived in and would tell the tale of the witch and the part of the creek that she'd turned into a circle. They would tell how she and her sister had a fight over a fellow they both liked. Fena, being the stronger of the two, turned her sister Minerva into a strange creature that lived in the creek near their home. People all around the area had reported seeing a woman with a tail like a mermaid swimming there, but no one actually knew if this was true or not.

Every time Aunt Sylvia would take someone out to the creek, I would try to tag along but she would always catch me and send me home. She didn't like me around too much while trying to tell the tall tales of Colby Point. She said I was too inquisitive and talked a mile a minute. I thing that she would like to tell the stories her way without too many interruptions.

Anyway, the walk took me and Sylvee only about five minutes, then Sylvee took a sharp right turn through some brush. It was sticky rose, and it hurt when you got too close to the flowers. I thought I saw some poison ivy to the left of me, and made sure that I watched where I was walking.

I could hear a sound like water, so I said to Sylvee, "Are we almost there yet?"

Sylvee turned around and shushed me up. "No talkin' right now, okay? I will tell you when we can talk!"

Suddenly, I could see a green-colored pond, and I was shocked to see that the legend was true. There was a round creek with a part of it that brought water in and a part of it that took water out to the Fox River. It swirled in a silent circular motion, like a whirlpool of sorts. Sylvee took me by the hand—and at this point I didn't care that hers was a dirty hand—and we stood right at the edge of the pond with our toes touching the soft ground near the water. I thought I saw something swimming in a circular motion and couldn't figure out why the fish was so long and big.

Sylvee let go of my hand and with a small step, she was ankle-deep in the pond. She held her dirty live treasure over the water and made a low clicking sound with her tongue.

"This is how I call Minerva. If you watch the top of the water, you will see her lips wait for the earthworm. I don't know if she will show herself completely because you're here. Just be real quiet and let me talk to her. And by the way, Minerva ain't no fish, she's a mermaid!"

I didn't even nod because I knew that I was about to see something that I had only heard about in the stories that Grandpa told me about the sea.

Sylvee talked real low and slow. She talked to some fish-like lips that bobbed in and out of the water, wanting the warm, wiggly worms that she held in the air for them. Each time Sylvee held out a worm, she would lift it just a bit higher in the air so that Minerva would be coaxed out a little more and more. I was mesmerized by this give-and-take that I was watching.

Suddenly, Minerva rose out of the water.

I saw a head like ours only smaller, and I saw that she was a greenish color and that she looked like a person, but I guess she could have been a huge fish. She continued to come farther and farther out of the water, until all of a sudden, I could see that she had hands that were webbed and very dark looking. I had stepped back in surprise when Minerva showed herself and had no idea that Irene Myatt was standing close behind me. I accidently stepped on her foot, which hurt her so much that she shoved me straight into the water!

Even though I was in the water, I could hear Sylvee yelling at Irene who was crying and yelling back that I'd hurt her foot. Once I came back up for air, all I could see was a huge, long, wide tail going deeper in the pond and out into the river, and I was being pulled along by the current to follow whatever it was.

"Hang on, Margie!" Sylvee yelled. "Just dog-paddle yourself to the Fox, and I will go get your grandpa to catch you as you drift by. Just keep paddling!"

I had no control of the situation and did exactly what Sylvee told me to do. I dog-paddled and kept telling myself that Minerva was gone and fish and turtles and snakes were all that were in the river. The circular motion of the water made me dizzy, but all of a sudden I was floating down a long creek that took me to a waterfall that poured me into the Fox River. I was helpless and couldn't get close enough to the shore to gain my footing. I knew how to keep afloat, so I decided that I might as well relax and try to stay alive.

First I floated by Ma Myatt standing on their broken pier. She waved and smiled at me. Next I floated past Peggy's house. She was on her tree swing that swung out over the river. She sat there with her mouth wide open, while I smirked at her because truly, I was having an adventure and she wasn't.

I turned myself around so I could see our riverfront and Mr. Boldt's pier next door. I thought to myself that if I tried really hard to stretch up my arms, I could maybe reach the bottom board of the pier and stop myself from floating too far down the river. Besides, I was getting tired and cold and just wanted to be on dry land. On our river shore, I could see Sylvee, my three aunts, and my grandpa all watching for me. Grandpa had taken off his shirt and shoes and was down to his undershorts, and Aunt Sylvia was trying to push the rowboat out so she could reach me before I went too far down the river.

Part of me got really scared, and part of me felt good to see all my family trying to help me. I was close to the pier, and I mustered up all my strength and tried to stretch to reach the end of it. But I was too short, too far away. Suddenly, just as I was floating by the pier with a heavy heart, I felt something come up from behind me and lift me out of the water. I mean, I was lifted up high enough to grab hold of the board! I hung on for dear life and tried to turn my head to see what or who had rescued me, but all I saw was the large tail of a fish. At least, it looked like a fish, but it was as long as I could stretch my arms out. I just stared and watched that thing swim away.

Suddenly, I felt the warm hard grip of Grandpa's hands. He pulled me straight up and started hugging me and yelling at me all at once. The three aunts came up with a towel that they wrapped around me. I was shaking so hard that I couldn't talk yet, and I remember them saying that I was in shock.

I was aware of Sylvee, though, and what she was doing. She gave me the thumbs-up and then walked away, back the way I'd come, dropping worms along the knee-deep water at the river's edge, calling her beloved Minerva home to the circle pond.

As we all walked toward home, Peggy came running up and just about knocked me over. "I am so sorry, Margie! I am glad that you are okay. After you dry off, do you want to play some dolls?"

Grandpa responded quickly, "That sounds real nice of you, Peggy. Why don't you come up while Margie gets changed, and Grandma will make you both some lemonade and cookies?" Life settled down again and before we knew it, Peggy and I were back into our usual routine of friends one week, fighting the next.

Sylvee and I had shared a special moment, and we now had a bond between us. I learned that she was real smart. I made sure that I always kept a handful of earthworms that Grandpa Bill dug up for fishing each day. I'd leave them on the doorstep of the Myatt's house for Sylvee to take to the circle pond. I didn't go back to the circle pond until many years later. I have longed for the confidence that Sylvee had when it came to the pond.

The day I visited the pond again, I grabbed some worms and dirt from my son's fishing gear. I put it in my pocket just like Sylvee did. I walked slowly into the darkened forest, and just like when I was young, I got cut by the thorn bushes, and I saw the poison ivy nearby. The area was much more overgrown, and I knew that no one had been back since the Myatts moved away. I tried to recall the chirping noise Sylvee had made with her mouth and the low tone she used while calling Minerva to the top of the pond.

Taking off my shoes and socks, I stood ankle-deep in the water. I have to admit that I was a bit scared and was watching out for other things like snakes and bloodsuckers, so I wasn't really looking down at the top of the pond where I was dangling a big, fat earthworm. All of a sudden, I heard a gurgling noise and right under my worm were some lips. Now, they could have been fish lips, but maybe they weren't. I wasn't brave enough to find out, and I wasn't foolish enough to tell anyone. Miracles like Minerva need to be protected and allowed to just be.

Gaining my confidence and remembering the long trip I had taken fifty years earlier through the pond and down the Fox River, I held out my hand and let the entire bunch of worms drop into the water. There was a flurry of bubbles and then a circular movement below. Just for a second, I thought I saw her face again.

Creeping backward and making sure that I wasn't going to step on Irene again (just kidding!), I said out loud, "I never got to thank you, Minerva, for saving my life. I have had a whole life because of you, and I promise never to allow anyone to disturb yours. Your secret is safe with me." Since that day I have told this story to my grandkids, and I promised them that one day if they were really good, I would take them to see the magical place where I found Minerva. I can't say whether she is still there or not, but there is no harm in believing.

Keep a sign in front of your imagination that says DO NOT DISTURB, because with fairy tales, anything is possible.

Chapter Seven

Silent Night

When Joseph and Mary got to Bethlehem, there was no place for them to stay because the inn was already full. They ended up spending the night in a stable, a place where animals were kept. There was fresh hay on the floor that they used for beds. That night, Jesus was born. There was no crib, so they laid the baby Jesus in a manger, which was actually a feeding trough for the animals. That night, some shepherds were in the fields near Bethlehem, keeping watch over their flocks of sheep. An angel appeared to them and gave them the good news that a Savior, the Messiah, had been born. The angel told the shepherds they could find Jesus lying in a manger. Suddenly a whole group of angels appeared saying, "Glory to God in the highest, and on earth peace, goodwill toward men!"

Paraphrased from Matthew 1–2 and Luke 1–2

I was a curious child. At eight and a half who wouldn't be when you have only your own imagination most of the time to keep you company? Life for me was grand and sad and an adventure, all wrapped up into one. My days of churchgoing began at the young age of four. I went faithfully with my aunts when they were in town, but in the months that they were gone, not so much. School was fun and a distraction of sorts. I made friends but they all lived so far away and my grandparents were too old to do the usual things that parents did. When I was at school I always felt like a visitor. I figured that it was something I had to do but that my real life was back in Colby Point at the end of the dirt road.

Eight years old is a strange age as it borders on a different level of understanding. As I sat and wondered what I was supposed to do my Grandpa Bill did something that I had no idea he could do. He made a nativity scene out of soft wood. He loved to whittle. He told me that it was a lost art, and that the world would be a better place if more people whittled instead of running their mouths off at one another. In case you do not know what whittling is, it is the art of carving something, of shaping something into something new. It usually means carving wood, but Grandma used to say that with all of my grandpa's teaching, he was whittling me into a fine human being.

Thanksgiving was over with, and this year my aunts had decided to stay for the winter. That was going to be great as it would break up the monotony of being at the end of the road all by ourselves. There would be daily coffee with Aunt Dula when she came up to gossip with Grandma. Aunt Lily would make her famous caramel cake for the Christmas party that we would go to at my cousin's house this year. I couldn't go too often when I was little because Grandpa wouldn't travel that far and leave Grandma alone for that long. Aunt Sylvia and Grandpa would meet in each other's garage, working on their cars, looking at things to fix in their homes, and listening to football games as the Bears went on to win that year.

Aunt Malita lived right next door to us, and she was a great traveler. She was a widow, and since her husband, my Uncle John Rhinelander, had passed, she traveled all over the world. I asked her why she went away so much, and she said that if she kept her feet moving, her heart wouldn't know that she was alone. That puzzled me, because she had all of us, but eventually I understood that she missed Uncle John. Aunt Malita was really a cousin to Grandpa and his sisters who lived right across the street.

The four of them never had children of their own, so they all kind of shared me. I had a great time and just loved the sound of all their voices. They made the small, quiet world that I lived in seem full and very busy.

The weeks flew by and soon it was the December twenty-third. Late in the day, Aunt Sylvia came up and told my grandparents that Aunt Malita had surprised them with a Christmas gift of a cruise, and they all were leaving in the morning. Grandpa and Grandma sounded so happy and excited for them. They talked about the sights they would see, and Aunt Sylvia promised to take many pictures for them.

She turned to me and said, "I'm sorry that we won't be here to take you to the party at the cousins' house, but we will next year. I promise!"

I was very disappointed, but I knew my grandmother expected me to mind my manners, so I simply nodded and said, "Have a nice trip." I turned and got my hat and coat on and called for Tinkerbell, and we went outside for a walk. I felt absolutely alone. I was angry and sad and so darn lonely. I walked and walked until I got to my valley. Tinker couldn't keep up and went back to the house, so I was by myself and able to sort out my thoughts.

It was my place, even at eight years old, to talk to God. I asked him why I was alone all the time. I asked him why I had no sisters or brothers and what I was supposed to do with myself. I asked him why everyone always left me and who was I supposed to be if I was never around anyone except my grandparents. There was no answer back except for the beating of my own heart and the taste of the salty tears on my lips as they ran down my cheeks. After a while, I heard Grandpa calling me with my Oscar Mayer whistle. It was time to come in, so I composed myself, then picked up some pinecones and some beautiful silver leaves from a birch tree that stood frozen from the ice storm we'd had the night before. I held up a leaf and examined the lines in it. They connected to one another and then finally to the stem. *All together,* I thought to myself.

I was beginning to feel better as I neared the house and went into the garage where Grandpa was having a smoke. He grinned when he saw me. "Hey there. What did you find in your secret place?" Puffs of blue smoke came from his lips.

I held them up for him to see and said, "Just some birch leaves that are frozen from the ice. I thought they would be pretty for the Christmas mantle."

"Yup, that is a good one to place there. Did you know the birch tree was around back when Jesus was born? Have you ever heard this story before?"

I nodded that I had and really didn't show an interest, but he said, "After we have supper and grandma makes some of her best hot chocolate, I have something I want you to help me with. I will tell you the Christmas story while we do it, if you'd like." That perked me up, but then I remembered the aunts.

"But when do you have to close up the aunts' house for their time away?"

He inhaled a long drag of his small cigarette and said, "Don't worry 'bout that, sweetie, there's time enough for that. They don't leave until tomorrow anyway. Let's you and me and Old Ironsides in there enjoy our night, okay?" It always made me laugh when he would call her "Old Ironsides" as she was in a wheelchair, and well, there was no delicate way to handle a marriage, I guess, that had survived almost fifty years.

I felt lighter and was glad that Grandpa could make it all right again. I walked into the warm kitchen and saw that Grandma had made double chocolate cupcakes and that she'd left the frosting bowl and wooden spoon for me. I hadn't even had supper yet. but in our home, dessert was considered not only a treat but a healing of the spirit. I sat down and licked the bowl clean.

When I was done, Grandma asked, "Do you have room for supper?" I smiled with chocolate all over my chin.

"I sure do!"

"Then go get washed up and changed, and then we will eat, have some hot chocolate, and Grandpa will tell you the Christmas story, if that's okay?"

"Okay?" I hollered. "It's wonderful!" Tinker started her barking and any sign of sadness was gone from our little home at the end of the street that night. Once supper was done and we all got into our respective places, Grandpa carried in a brown shoebox. He lit the hurricane lamp, then turned off the electric lights to make our small living room feel like one from days gone by—before man had made it modernized, as he would say.

Grandpa started pulling little pieces of a nativity scene out of the box. I gasped at the beauty of them. Each piece was a beautiful, soft, blond wood, carved by Grandpa and finished with strokes of love. There were Joseph and Mary and the stable animals, a small trough with hay in it, and a tiny baby Jesus. How Grandpa had managed to carve the three wise men so precisely amazed me. One by one, he placed them on our narrow living room wall table among the beautiful silver birch leaves that I had found, and as he did, he shared the story with Grandma and me. We listened as if we had never heard that story before, and even Tinker sat in complete contentment at the sound of Grandpa's voice. He drew me in—I was there with Mary and Joseph on their travels. I felt the anticipation of being on the road alone, the anxiety as they had no place to lay their heads. I was worried for a split second that Mary would not find a place to have baby Jesus but then blushed because I knew that story.

On and on Grandpa went, until Jesus was born and the three wise men were kneeling all around them as they all witnessed the miracle of the Christmas birth. When he finished, I was jolted back to reality, and I could see the tears falling from Grandma's eyes. It felt good to see the softer side of her as she often had to harden her shell a bit. Not being able to walk made her dependent on us, and that was something she said life was trying to teach her not to resent. It was time for bed, and I hugged Grandma and Grandpa and went to my room with Tinkerbell close to my side.

I could hear them talking in the other room while Grandpa got her undressed and into bed. There was such trust and love in our home, and as I fell asleep, I knew that I was very lucky indeed. The night went by slowly and I dreamt that I was in a storm and that the wind was howling and that our windows were rattling to its force.

In an instant, I was really awake. I looked outside of my window and there was a storm going on! The snow was blowing up and around in the wind, and the tree branches were becoming heavy under wet snow. I smelled the breakfast smell of their coffee and didn't bother to get dressed. I ran into the kitchen and jumped as I stepped into a puddle of wet snow and ice. Grandpa had had to get up early and help the aunts dig out so they could drive all the way to the airport in Chicago. They had to make it before the storm grounded them from the trip that they were taking.

"It's cold out there, and that snow ain't a-stoppin'." Grandpa shouted, even though we could hear him just fine.

Grandma saw the look on my face and my feet in the puddle, and she said above Grandpa's chatter, "Get dressed, Margie, and for goodness sake, make sure your feet are dry before you put your socks and shoes on!"

I went back into the room that I shared with Grandpa and dressed in my long johns and heavy socks. I got out my snowsuit and boots, as I intended to make a fort out there. I was sure if I made it big enough, then Joey and Theresa Bach would come down this way for a snowball fight. Theresa was a bit younger than me, and Joey was a bit older. We played together when the weather allowed us to, but lately winter had kept us to our respective parts of the street. I ate my breakfast in haste and went outside. I was in awe at how the majestic storm had covered everything in sight with its glorious snow. I knew not to say that in front of Grandpa, as he grumbled quite loudly at the work that he had ahead of him.

After about thirty minutes, I had had enough. The storm was really getting fierce, and the temperature was beginning to drop. I walked alongside the garage where the snow was the deepest— almost to my thighs. I managed to get into the garage through the back door and then began the long process of cleaning off before I went into Grandma's kitchen. As I walked in, I could hear the radio announcer going on about the ten to twelve inches of snow that was hitting northern Illinois, especially near the Fox River. That was it for my day outside and any hope to have fun with some friends. I changed into warm, dry clothes and cuddled up next to Grandpa, who was on our big green couch doing a crossword puzzle.

"Had enough of outside, have you?" he asked.

"Yes I have, and I just want to stay warm and read my book." They had given me the book *Stormy* the year before, and I must have read it ten times already.

"Well, that's good, Margie. You just settle down, and we will make our way to the aunts' house tomorrow after this storm eases up. Besides, it's nice to see a light on across the street, ain't it?"

I must have been sleepy because I don't remember even reading my book. I simply fell asleep and dreamt I was riding on a horse next to Mary and Joseph. The story was still so strong with me that it drew my mind and thoughts back to the miracle that was given to us.

Later on into the evening after supper, we were all watching television. Grandpa had on *Bonanza*, and I loved that there were brothers on a ranch together. I would say to them while we watched the show that someday I was going to have a son as big as Hoss Cartwright. Grandpa would shake his head and ask me why I would want that, but Grandma would smile and say "From your lips to God's ears, Margie."

Our show ended, which was my cue to get ready for bed. We were all still sitting there in our warm, quiet house safe from the storm outside, when all of a sudden we saw lights coming down our snow-covered gravel road. The car was moving slowly, and at first I wondered if the aunts had missed their plane because of the storm. Grandpa got up and watched through our window and Tinkerbell climbed up on the big red chair next to him.

"That's not the aunts' car," Grandpa said aloud.

"Well, who'd be out in a storm like this, Bill?" Grandma asked. As we all watched, the car stopped right in front of the aunts' house, and a thin, younger-looking man came running to our front door. He banged on our screen door, and Grandpa went to open it. Before he could ask what was wrong, the man came in and in his broken English told us that they were on their way to the hospital in McHenry and had gotten lost. His wife was having a baby, and now he didn't have time to get there and, well...could we help them? My grandparents both were taken by surprise and for just a moment stood there and said nothing at all.

So I chirped up and said, "This is just like the Christmas miracle that you told us about, Grandpa! You can help them, can't you?" That was all that they needed to hear.

Grandpa took the man by the hand and said, "Hold on, young fella, we have a place for you and your wife to stay; she will be just fine. You go to her, and I will be right there." The stranger turned and ran all the way back to his car. I could see them talking and him comforting her.

"Have you ever helped birth a child, Bill?" Grandma asked.

"Nope, just animals on the farm, Cleo," he replied.

"Well, that's good enough. It will have to be." Grandma looked at me and said, "You have to help Grandpa and these strangers with their miracle, okay? You get dressed and go over, and then I will call you on the aunts' phone. You tell Grandpa everything I tell you, and there will be no problems at all. You're a big girl, and here is a miracle you can see with your own eyes."

Following her instructions, I left Tinker with Grandma and carried the torn sheets that we had for emergency cuts and the mercurochrome that we used for antiseptic across the street. I could feel my heart pounding as I followed the three adults into my aunts' house. It felt surreal to be in their home with strangers but without them. I set everything down on Aunt Sylvia's dresser and waited for Grandma to call as she promised she would.

While I waited, I had a chance to study these two strangers. They were not very old—in fact, they were kind of young to be parents already, I thought to myself. The lady had long brown hair that was wet with snow and sweat, I assumed. She was breathing hard and speaking in a language that I didn't understand. Her husband spoke our language, but not well. He was so worried, and he kept calling my grandfather "mister." I almost laughed out loud when heard him call him that.

My grandfather came into the room and stopped the man. "My name is Bill," he said, and he enunciated the way to say his name.

"Be-i-lll," the young man said over and over. Grandpa kept repeating it until he finally had it right. I jumped as the loud shrill of the phone snapped me back to reality. It was Grandma on the other end, of course.

"Margie, I need you to be really strong, you hear me?"

"Yes, I will." I answered back.

She continued on. "Now tell Grandpa that he needs to look at her private area to see if he can see the baby's head or not. Okay, Margie?"

I stuttered out an okay and walked up to Grandpa and whispered in his ear, as I thought that was kind of a private thing to say.

"No time to be squeamish," he said to me. "You've seen the puppies born at the Walkers' house when their dog had her time, remember? So this is not different. She's just a different species of one of God's beings, that's all."

With that, I felt very assured that I could help, and it went just the way my grandparents told me it would. I told Grandpa word for word what to do, and he did it. The young man stayed by his wife's side holding her hand and helping her breathe. It seemed to go so quickly, and all of a sudden there was a new life born right out on Aunt Sylvia's bed.

Boy, is she going to be upset, I thought as I laughed through my tears. They had a little boy, all pink and screaming so loud that it hurt my ears. I looked around and saw that all the adults including Grandpa were crying. He took the baby and cleaned him up and handed him to his mother.

Grandpa sent me home and said, "I am going to make sure that they are cleaned up and safe for the night." I turned to leave, but then he grabbed my arm and said, "Guess we were supposed to be here instead of a party, huh?"

I must have had my mouth wide open, because he took his index finger and gently pushed it shut as he laughed and said, "You'd better learn to take life's surprises and miracles in stride, or you will be walking around your entire life with your mouth hangin' open. That's not a good thing to do, 'cause you'll swallow bugs!"

He made me laugh, and at that moment I knew that I had a purpose and that God had answered my questions from our conversation back in my valley the day before. I was never really alone, and if I just trusted in him and Grandma, I would be a really good human being.

The next day, the young couple brought the little baby over with them, and we all sat together and had a Christmas breakfast. It was nice and fun, and Tinker never barked once as she sat and stared at the little baby sleeping on the couch next to me. While the grown-ups talked, I got to babysit a little. I touched his fingers and smelled his skin. I knew that someday I would have a bunch of these miracles, as I wanted all the fun and noise of wonderful human beings around me as they came to Mother Earth.

Almost a year went by, and our warm summer quickly turned into fall. Thinking about that special night, I had almost forgotten that Grandpa and I went out and bought a brand new mattress for Aunt Sylvia, and she never knew that there was a miracle in her bed. She kept telling Grandpa that she'd never realized how good her bed here felt until she was gone from it.

As fall slipped away, the first snow came in all its beauty. Soon we had a Christmas tree in our front room, and we were going through last year's treasures and decorations. I opened up the brown box and held the beautiful wooden pieces that Grandpa had made for us the year before. Suddenly a car came down the road.

"Looks like another stranger took a wrong turn," Grandpa said to us. We waited for the car to turn around, but instead it parked in our driveway. A young man got out and went around to the other side. A woman holding a little boy about a year old got out, and they walked toward our house. My grandparents looked at each other and waited until there was a soft knock on the door.

As Grandpa opened up the door, Grandma said to me, "It's them—it's our Christmas Miracle, come for a visit!" They came in and there were greetings all around.

I shouted through the noise, "What did you name your little boy?"

The man looked at Grandpa and said, clear as a bell, "Bill."

There was a hush in our home, a moment of knowing the gift of being human and being together. I didn't want that moment to end, but all things do end.

Grandpa laughed and said, "Well, I'll be."

Grandma said, "That's a good name," at the same time, and Tinker barked and barked and turned in circles.

The adults went into the kitchen as little Bill and I sat on the floor near the front of the Christmas tree. He seemed to know me and liked touching the things I had out. Reaching into the box, he pulled out the baby Jesus from our nativity scene. He held it and rolled it around in his hands. I sat closer and started taking out all the pieces.

As he watched me, I said, "Would you like me to tell you the story about the Christmas Miracle?" Bill laughed, and I remembered to tell it to him word for word. We had the best of times, and I was able to remember the glory of it all—the night I saw the birth of one of God's beings—and I remembered the words of the song we sang on Christmas Eve.

Silent night, holy night
All is calm, all is bright.
Round yon virgin mother and Child.
Holy Infant so tender and mild,
Sleep in heavenly peace, Sleep in heavenly peace.

Chapter Eight

CARRIE AND THE CHOCOLATE WELL

I love chocolate sweet and low, the taste, the name, the smell
I loved it even more that day with Carrie in the well
She fell you see not deep and down yet deep enough to see
Hands that help her strong and safe while simply watching me
I carried each delicious can and smelled the nectar deep
With watering mouth and sticky hands I wanted this to keep.
I held my breath as pour they must upon her head below
I stood and stared mouth open wide while simply saying "no!"
But when they pulled the mighty one from well so deep and long
The chocolate sprayed all over me, I sang a different song.
"It's raining chocolate" I did yell with every savory swallow
And worry not if chocolates gone because there is tomorrow.

∾

*I*t was the early fall of 1963 and I was 9. Everyone in our small neighborhood was getting ready for the upcoming winter season. There were leaves to burn, windows and doors to caulk, and baking to be done. If you took the time to walk past the houses on our street, you would smell a mix of cinnamon bread, pumpkin pie, and all things chocolate. I loved chocolate as a child—still do! My grandmother always said that if she wanted me to try something, all she had to do was dip it in chocolate syrup first. I sure am glad that I had understanding and smart grandparents when it came to my love of chocolate.

Anyway, this particular fall, our neighbors, Carrie and Irv Medlinger, had decided that they would like to bake for the fall festival that was being held in nearby Island Lake. The church that we all went to there had a huge field, and someone had donated a very large circus tent to the town, so the church council decided to put it to good use. They announced there would be a carnival in town, along with music and a contest for the best sugar cookie in McHenry County.

That was all Carrie had to hear! We all knew in Colby Point that Carrie Medlinger made not just an ordinary sugar cookie; she made a *chocolate* sugar cookie. That was rare, as all throughout time, women from all generations claimed to have the best *vanilla* sugar cookie around.

After a rainy week, it was nice to see the sun out and feel a bit of warmth still left in the breeze. In fact, Grandma Cleo was working on her own variation of a vanilla sugar cookie, so Grandpa Bill sort of suggested that I go outside with Tinkerbell and see what I might find in the way of colored leaves and fall treasures. Huge oak and maple trees surrounded our property, as well as our silver birch trees, and the fall colors were very bright that year.

I took my wooden basket that I used for finding treasures and thankfully escaped from kitchen duties. I heard Grandma Cleo ask Grandpa Bill where I was off to, and he simply said I was treasure hunting. I found so many beautiful leaves that my basket grew full in no time. The colors made me feel warm and special inside. It was amazing, but as I studied each leaf, there were no two alike!

I grabbed some plump acorns that the squirrels had missed and some pinecones too.

Walking to the edge of our yard, I saw some pretty yellow leaves along the road in front of the Boldt's house. I was allowed to go all the way to the Medlinger's, so I wasn't worried about breaking any rules. In fact, the closer I got, the more I could smell the sweet, intoxicating aroma of chocolate. It made my mouth water, and my eyes began to tear up. Even Tinkerbell stopped with one paw up in the air, sniffing to see where she could find some morsels.

All of a sudden, the garage door of Carrie and Irv's house opened up with a rush, and Irv came out. I must have jumped a foot because Irv began to laugh as he walked toward me. He couldn't help but see me standing there, obviously enjoying the smells drifting out from Carrie's kitchen. Irv was a small and stout-looking German man. He had twinkling blue eyes and very dark skin from always working outside in the garden and around his pier on the Fox River.

Next thing I knew, Irv had his arms around me and was giving me a bear hug. He tickled me at the same time, and I have to admit I loved the attention. Having a sick grandma and an elderly grandfather, neither of them had too much strength for picking me up and hugging me like Irv could. Sometimes when his daughter Sophie would come out with her kids, Suzie and Oscar, I would sit at the end of my driveway and watch as the family would rush together in a flurry of excitement and love. I liked to pretend that I was them for as long as I could, and I did that in this moment.

My make-believe family was complete for a moment, until Irv's sudden, "Hey, what are you up to, Margie?" woke me from my daydream.

Tinkerbell twirled in a circle and barked as if to say, "We are here for chocolate, and you know that!" Grandma Cleo always said, "You never ask, Margie. You wait to be asked." So not wanting to be too forward, I waved my hands at Tinkerbell to make her hush.

"Shh, Tinker! Hello, Irv. I was just wondering if I could visit with Carrie for a spell?"

There was a sudden loud crash, and both Irv and I turned toward the house to see what it was. It seemed to come from behind the house, down by the river shore. "That was a loud noise," Irv said, scratching his head. But there was no sound after, so we both just shrugged it off.

"I am on my way down to see Mr. Bach and then possibly off to the store again for Carrie. I will be back, so you just let the two of you in. I am sure that Carrie is waitin' on your visit," he said with a gentle shove toward the front door.

As Irv walked down the gravel road, I could almost swear I heard someone calling his name from far away. But that couldn't be, since the only people in the house were Carrie and me and, of course, Tinkerbell. I walked into the breezeway and, as always, was taken aback by all the dark cherry wood that they loved so much. They didn't just use it for the floor but for their walls and ceilings throughout the house, too. Even the twin rocking chairs were made of the same wood.

Carrie made all her own chair covers and curtains. She changed them each season. For the fall, they were transformed from a lazy sunflower pattern to one of pumpkins, gourds, and leaves in various colors of fall. I touched her curtains and knew that someday I would learn how to sew. I would be a wife and a mother to a houseful of children, and my children would have a father that came home, and we would be a complete family just like the Medlingers were. I was completely lost in yet another wishful daydream, when I heard a very weak sounding voice calling what sounded to me like "help."

I hurried through the breezeway door into the huge warm kitchen, fully expecting to find Carrie sitting on her stool baking away at her famous chocolate sugar cookies, but she was nowhere to be found. I saw huge bags of flour and sugar and a can of chocolate syrup the size of my head or maybe bigger. I remembered that Grandma Cleo had told me Carrie and Irv lived during the Great Depression, just like my grandparents did, and because of this, once Carrie and Irv had money, they always bought the biggest size of anything that they used a lot of. It was actually less expensive and gave Carrie a sense of security.

Suddenly, I saw smoke coming from the oven. Remembering what I'd seen Carrie do a hundred times before, I put on her oven gloves and opened the door to take out the burning cookies. The tray was much hotter than I'd anticipated and I could feel the burning heat through the glove. Startled, I dropped the whole thing on the floor. Then I almost turned and ran home, when all of a sudden, I heard that cry for help again. This time I was sure it was coming from Carrie, but I walked through the house and couldn't find her.

Tinkerbell was scratching at the back door that led to the river, so I opened up the door and she was gone in a flash. Pushing past the sound of my grandfather's voice in my head warning me not to go to the river unsupervised, I stepped out. That is when I saw a huge hole in the ground. There used to be a well there, but Carrie and Irv had covered it as it only gave them mud. They had dug a new one, and this one was supposed to be filled in, but they never got around to it.

"Help me, please, whoever is up there. Margie, is that you?"

Oh my! It was Carrie, and she had fallen through the wooden plank and into the mud well! I walked over as Tinker barked and barked. "I will get help, Carrie. Are you okay?"

"Yes, I think so, but I cannot get out. I may have broken my ankle. Please go get Irv and turn off my oven, please?" I nodded and ran toward the Bach's house that was next down the street. At the same time, my grandfather was out cutting our front lawn, and he looked up to see me running really fast down the road. I was screaming for Irv at the top of my lungs, and he heard me. Grandpa starting running from our direction, and Irv came running from the other direction. Irv got there first, and gaining my composure, I explained what I'd found. He took off to his house. Just then Grandpa showed up, and we also ran to the back of Carrie and Irv's house.

The three of us peered down at poor Carrie, all talking at once. Tinkerbell continued barking loudly. Carrie held up one hand to shush us. "I am okay. Irv, you need to be calm in this situation. Please get on the phone and call Sheriff Fino and get some help."

Irv immediately called Sheriff Fino who came in a hurry, followed by the town's tow truck. Fred Ferguson—the man with the tow truck—said he had seen just about everything until he saw Carrie. He stood there scratching his head and thinking on how he could pull her out without hurting her any more than she already was.

Sheriff Fino walked toward the well and said, "Too bad we can't just drop an inner tube in there, put it around her, and pull her out." They dropped the tire down the well, she put it around herself, and it would have worked, but the mud had already dried around her. She was really stuck.

She was beginning to get upset when all of a sudden I said, "Too bad we couldn't make her slippery like a chocolate sundae. Chocolate makes everything go down easier."

All four men stopped what they were doing and looked at me.

"I think the girl has an idea," said Irv. He asked Grandpa and Sheriff Fino to go to the shed with him. When they walked back, each man had a gigantic, opened can of chocolate syrup. Irv explained to Carrie that they could always get more chocolate, but to get her out, she needed to be slippery.

Now, I love chocolate, but not enough to pour it on myself. I watched in complete amazement as each can was poured on and around Carrie, who instinctively began to eat it as it ran down her head onto her face and neck. In fact, Carrie ate so much of it that she began to laugh and that made her body relax. Right at that moment, Sheriff Fino told Fred Ferguson to give that tire a pull. And do you know what happened next?

That tire started moving up, and as Carrie's body began to move, the pressure began to mount. More and more the tire pulled, until suddenly there was a loud sound like a suction cup. *Pop!* went the well, and Carrie flew up in the air. Everything and everyone became covered in warm gooey chocolate. Carrie was freed from the tire and placed gently on the ground. She was okay, but she did have a broken ankle. Just then, the ambulance from McHenry Hospital drove up, and two men in white clothes came running to Carrie and helped her get on a stretcher.

This was really something—I had never seen an ambulance come down our street before, and when they turned on the siren as they left, it was so loud that Tinkerbell began to howl. Irv called us later that evening and said that the doctor wanted to make sure that there were no other injuries for Carrie, so she had to stay the night. Irv told Grandpa that it was the first time in over forty years that they were not sleeping in the same bed. Grandpa said that we had a really nice couch that he was welcome to use if he couldn't sleep tonight, but Irv declined and said that he had all the cookies to put away and sample.

Early the next morning, the phone rang. It was Carrie, and she wanted me to come down for a visit. Irv had picked her up, and she was anxious to see me. My grandparents said it was okay, and Tinkerbell and I were at her house in a flash. All the way to her house, I tried to think of things to ask her about the ride in the ambulance. I wanted to make sure that I wasn't being too nosey, because Grandma always told me, "If people want you to know something, they will tell you without you being nosey!"

We had a great visit talking and laughing about her chocolate adventure. I was happy that she was okay and even more thankful that before her fall, she had made ten dozen of her chocolate sugar cookies.

Irv came in with a box full of them and said, "These are for you and your family...and here's a bone for Tinker." As I walked home, I thought of how an ordinary day turned out to be an adventure and also a lesson. I learned that life is what you make of it, and if you are lucky...it will be sweet.

Chapter Nine

SECRET SANTA

Now that the ice is on the pond
And skaters come and go
The cheeks turned red at nightfall
Not warmed in fallen snow.
Just as the fields are white with frost
And trees of Christmas have come
All children nestled into their beds
As the presents come undone...

*G*rowing up in a blended family such as ours had its perks. I had my grandparents' stability and structure, mixed in with the magic and miracles of life that were given to me like precious jewels as I grew up. I also had my mother who was a pianist and because of work had to live in Chicago. We went shopping together sometimes, and she always brought me the most beautiful clothes. I admit it was hard to leave her after a visit, and there were a few days of tears and sulking, but sooner or later I would be able to move past it and accept what life had handed to me. Grandma always said that when life hands you lemons, you make lemonade!

Christmas of 1963 was a very special Christmas. My three aunts across the street stayed home that winter, and my mother came to stay with us for Christmas. Nothing could have made this holiday more special than having all the excitement of family together again. Because our house was so small, my mother and I got to share a bedroom, and Grandpa graciously slept on the extra couch in Grandma's room. It was like camping out, he said.

As we were waiting for Mom to arrive, Grandpa mopped the bathroom floor, and I dusted all the tables, pictures, and knick-knacks scattered throughout the living room. I was careful not to break anything as each treasure had a meaning to Grandma. There were the small doves that Aunt Malita brought to her from California and the lovely clock from Germany that the aunts across the street gave her. I was proud of our little home and couldn't wait to share it with my mother.

It was strange to know that I would have three whole days with her here, and I wasn't going to waste a moment of them. Grandma had used the day before to make tons of cookies. There were cutout sugar cookies, crescent moons, and fudge. Grandma's cookies were great, but her fudge was the best! She had a secret recipe that only I was allowed to watch, and when Aunt Dula came up snooping around, Grandma had me hide the three different types of chocolate in the bread drawer so that she couldn't see them. There was always a pot of coffee on the stovetop and warm bread on the back stove burner.

Aunt Dula came up for sweets and gossip, but Grandma wasn't having any of it that morning. After about ten minutes, Aunt Dula knew she wasn't getting anywhere and was about to leave when a taxicab pulled up. The door opened, and there stood my mother! She was a very slender, beautiful blonde. The driver helped her out and even brought in her bags into the house. She paid him and went to tip him, but he told her no and said, "Merry Christmas!"

I looked at her and I was immediately in her arms, hugging her as tight as I could. Aunt Dula greeted her and gave her the once-over to see how she looked and acted. Grandma wheeled into the room and bumped into Aunt Dula, who turned and left, kind of flustered.

Grandpa laughed as he hugged Mom and said, "Come on into my room, Joycie. You can have my bed, and I made room in the closet for your things." They walked arm and arm, and I watched as Grandma followed with a bit of a tear in her eyes. Once Mom had all her things put away, she called me into our room. A long white bag was hanging on the door.

Mom walked toward the bag and as she unzipped it, she said, "This is your Christmas dress that I had made for you, Margie. I hope you like the lavender color. It's two pieces with white tights and patent leather shoes." I must have gasped when she pulled it out, because she turned around and said, "What's wrong?"

My mother was considered legally blind due to a childhood illness, with only partial sight. Her left eye was completely blind and her right eye had some calcium covering the eye in such a way that most people and things looked clouded. Yet, she still managed to look beautiful, and live a somewhat normal life. It was hard to understand at first, but living in a household where some of the adults had handicaps, I had learned quickly how to be extra careful when I explained what I was doing.

So I answered, "Nothing is wrong. I love it, and the color is perfect! I will be so excited to show it to Kyle and Debbie and Vickie tomorrow night!" Suddenly there was a knock on the door, and we went to the kitchen window to look out. It was a delivery man, and he had a huge box in his hands. I wondered who could have sent it.

Grandpa went to the door, and the delivery man said, "I have a delivery for a Margie Reiling. Can you sign for this, please?"

I looked at my mother for some hint that it was from her, but she said to Grandma, "I wonder if it's from Jack."

Well, I wasted no time, and with Grandpa's help, we got the box open. Inside was the most beautiful bouquet of red and white flowers I had ever seen. Grandpa took out the card and handed it to me. It said "Merry Christmas, darling. Love, your father, Jack R." This was a very touching moment, as my father had been away and I had not seen him for a few years. I caught a glimpse of my mother's face and it showed a very sad person, so I made up my mind that this would be a Christmas that she would remember forever. I had my mother here with me for a big party with family tomorrow night, and my father hadn't forgotten me after all.

I wondered to myself why everyone was so quiet, but then Grandpa stepped up and said, "Those are real nice flowers there from your dad. Let's put them on the piano so we can all enjoy them."

The only thing that made me sad right then was that Grandma Cleo could not go to the party. It was just across the street, and I begged and pleaded with her to let us try to wheel her down to the aunts' house. But it was to no avail.

"It's too cold for me to go outside, honey," she explained. "If I were to go out and get sick, I'd end up in the hospital. You remember what it was like, the last time I was gone, right?" I sure did. I gave up trying to push her too much. "Besides," she whispered to me, "I can travel there just fine. Remember that even though I cannot walk, it doesn't stop me from flying." Grandma had told me on more than one occasion all about a place she had been to without any of us. She described the trees and the houses and just everything about that place. She said that God might have taken away her legs, but he'd given her wings instead. Grandpa said he would walk down for a bit, but he didn't like to leave Grandma alone too long in case something should happen.

My mother had helped me put my hair all up in pin curls. Once I was all dressed in my new outfit, I could hardly wait for the time to go to the party. What joy! My lavender dress had a white ruffled apron that went around my body and tied in a beautiful white bow. My mother had me stand on the piano bench and my grandfather took a picture of me with my mothers new color camera, smelling the flowers that Jack had sent to me.

Finally, it was time! I put on my blue wool coat and my white hat and muff. Before we left, I spun around the room so my grandmother could see me.

"You will be the prettiest girl at the party, Margie, my darling! Don't forget that Santa Claus will be making a stop there tonight, so please be on your best behavior."

I stopped twirling because in all the excitement, I had almost forgotten to put out the plate of cookies for Santa, along with some carrots for his reindeer. I ran to the kitchen, but Grandpa already had it ready and handed it to me.

"Be sure you put it under the tree. That way when he gets here, he'll be sure to see it."

"I will, Grandpa. Thanks!" I was so excited. "Well, goodbye, Grandma!" I waved to her as she lay in her bed.

"Goodbye, Margie. Have fun and say hi to all the cousins for me, okay?"

"I will, I promise!"

Grandpa opened the door to walk me across the street, since my mother had already gone down to the aunts' to help set up the party. I stepped outside into the cold air and felt the crunch of the snow beneath my shoes. I looked up at the huge stars in the sky that looked just like diamonds.

I took in a deep breath and yelled, "Merry Christmas, Santa Claus!" so loudly that my grandfather jumped.

"You'll wake the dead with a shout like that, Margie!"

"I'm sorry, Grandpa. I just want to make sure that he doesn't forget to show up. I know how busy he is, going all over the world tonight."

As we neared my aunts' open garage door, I turned and looked back at my house. It looked warm and soft, and I could see perfectly into my front room. I felt lonely for Grandma but knew that she would be seeing all of this in her mind because she could fly.

As I walked in, there were so many people already there. My cousins Kyle, Kim, Scott, Todd, and Mark were sitting by the tree. Aunt Ruthie and Uncle Earl and their kids were there also. The energy was swirly and I looked for a place to sit down next to my cousins Vickie and Debbie. We nestled down together to await the arrival of Santa Claus and all the gifts that he would bring. I'd been really good that year, and I knew that he would not forget me.

All of a sudden, there was a banging on the side door to my aunts' house. I heard the jingling of reindeer bells and a deep, long, "Ho ho ho!"

"He's here!" We all shouted it, more than once. Aunt Phyllis had us get in line and make a path in the living room. Suddenly, with a wisp of cold air and some wet snow falling onto Aunt Dula's freshly cleaned floor, in walked Santa. He seemed a bit stooped over I thought, but at the same time he was carrying a very big bag of gifts. Another thing that bothered me was that I noticed that he had the same type of copper-buckled winter boots as my grandfather had. I decided maybe Grandpa and Santa both shopped at Montgomery Ward. I knew it was a very good store.

Now all my cousins were just as eager as I was, and they seemed to outnumber me. Mark, Scott, Kim, Kyle, and Todd quickly grabbed each other and pushed forward, as did Debbie, Craig, Vickie, Kurt, Sharon, and Keith. In a matter of moments, I found myself directly behind Santa, watching my cousins get their long-awaited gifts and staring at the back of his head. I watched for what seemed to be a long time, but then I saw something that knocked the wind out of me. Santa had the same eyeglass band that Grandpa Bill did, but that I knew he didn't get at Montgomery Ward. He got it from me! Right below his red furry hat, the band read *from Margie.*

I felt warm and sick to my stomach and wanted to go home. It wasn't hard to get away—I just kept slowly backing up past the outstretched hands and the loud chatter until I was in the dark safety of Aunt Dula's kitchen. I slipped into the breezeway and outside to the frigid air. It was all suddenly clear—there was no Santa Claus, and I had been lied to by the people I loved the most!

I ran as fast as I could into the night with the stars twinkling in the sky and the moon so full it was as if I had a lit path all the way home to our little house. I slipped and fell a few times because I was wearing my very best but slippery patent leather shoes, but I made it home. I pushed on the door hard, and it slammed into the wall. That startled Grandma Cleo, who was in bed listening to her transistor radio.

"What's wrong, child?" Grandma asked me. I went to her and lay across her bed and sobbed for a long time while her one good hand stroked the back of my head. She was still and warm, and all the time as she touched me, I felt waves of grief leaving me. After a bit I was able to take a deep breath, and she asked me again, "What happened that brought all these tears tonight?"

Sitting up, I said, "There's no Santa Claus, and you all lied to me. It's Grandpa down there—I saw the headband that I gave to him last year for his birthday and...and...when I saw it, I knew it was all a lie!"

As the tears started again, Grandma gently put her fingers under my chin, lifted my head, and said, "That is why you are crying? Don't you know that Santa has to have help? He surely could not be everywhere, no matter how much magic he has in him. Besides, take a look at the Christmas tree. There were no gifts there before you went to the party, but there are gifts there now, aren't there?"

I shook my head and said, "Anyone could have done that. There's no Santa Claus!" Grandma had a good way to let you sit and think about what you just said, so we sat there quietly for about ten minutes. Then she gave me a jiggle. I sat up and looked at her, and she had a tear coming down her cheek. I felt awful that I'd made her cry—I never wanted to do that. I was ashamed at my selfish, spoiled self.

"I am sorry, Grandma. If you believe there is a Santa Claus, then I do too! Please don't cry!"

"I am not crying because I do not believe. I am crying because *you* don't believe. Santa Claus is real, and he is in here"—she pointed to my chest. "He is in our thoughts, and he is our hope that magic does exists. Have I seen him? Yes, I have! I saw him provide food on a cold winter's day to a family that had none, from the goodness of a stranger who knew they were starving. Santa saw that need and made sure that it was filled. I saw him give hope to a mother whose child was ill. When Santa came to the hospital to visit that child, there was an improvement because that little child believed that if there really was a Santa Claus, then anything was possible, even getting well."

I stood up and had that *aha*! moment that comes into your life when suddenly you are aware of what just happened. I knew what she was trying to tell me, and that terrible desperation left me.

"Oh! I understand Grandma. In my heart I feel better, and I know it's because of the magic of Santa Claus."

With a beautiful smile on her face she said, "You're all grown up in one small moment...and you understand.... You are just like me." That was what I always wanted to hear, and it was the best present that anyone could have given to me!

"Now you go back and have fun," she told me. "Do not let on to the others, as it would hurt your cousins and most of all Grandpa would be so sad. Okay?"

"Okay," I whispered. I walked over to her and looked into her face and whispered, "I'm just like you." Kissing her, I turned and went back into the magical night, and I didn't run. I took my time looking up at the stars and moon. Not really paying attention to my surroundings, I was startled to hear the crunching of boots on the snow. Looking into the night toward my aunts' house and the party, I could see a figure coming toward me. Rubbing my eyes, I realized that it was Santa Claus—well, Grandpa, actually.

Giving it my best try, I would not let on that I knew who he really was. As we neared each other, he let out a "Ho, ho ho" and reached for my hands. "I looked all around for you, Margie, and you weren't there. Did you have to go somewhere that took you away from the party tonight?" I looked into his eyes, and they were so bright they almost twinkled like the stars above.

"I had to check on Grandma Cleo. I am sorry I missed the gift-giving tonight, Santa." I made sure I accentuated the word *Santa*.

Seeming bigger to me at the moment, Santa began to chuckle and said, "Well, young lady, your grandma and grandpa always let me know that you are the best little girl in the world.... Well, maybe not so little anymore, huh?" He rubbed my pink cheek from the cold. "Now you get into that house and enjoy your party. I left some really nice gifts for you tonight, but I have many places to be, so I have to fly!"

I hugged him—I just had to! I was so proud of my grandparents and what I had learned tonight. We both turned and began moving toward our destinations, when all of a sudden I couldn't hear the crunching of his boots anymore. I stopped and turned around—but he was gone!

What?? Where could he be? Even Grandpa isn't that light on his feet. I walked back to where we'd said our goodbyes, and looked at the ground. There were only a few more boot marks, and then they stopped. I ran around the house, but he wasn't there. I walked toward the road, and he wasn't there either. Then, as I looked up into the sky, I saw a flash. It was bright and long and seemed to go on forever. I followed that star and watched it fade from sight, standing there with my mouth open. What just happened? Could it be? Was that really....no, it couldn't be. But was it?

Smiling to myself and suddenly feeling the cold of the night, I decided that I did believe and turned and ran to the aunts' house. There in the warmth of family were my cousins and aunts and uncles. Everyone hugged me and asked me where I had gone.

My cousin Mark chirped up and said, "Too bad, Margie. You missed Santa Claus, you dummy!" That automatically got him in trouble with his mom and caused a bunch of laughter among the family. Just then the door opened, and Grandpa Bill walked in.

We immediately locked eyes as I said, "I didn't miss him, Mark. Santa is here"—I pointed to my chest—"always. He never leaves us, ever."

"Oh, brother," Mark said as he rolled his eyes.

Grandpa came and sat down by me and helped me open my gifts. It was a grand time with family and friends, a night that has stayed with me over fifty years. The most important lesson I learned that night was to believe—after all, there would be no Santa Claus without faith.

Chapter Ten

THE FOX RIVER, LUCKY, AND ME

End of the Road

There was a place that I grew up; it wasn't far from home.
The cars were far and few between, instead the deer did roam.
Our house was placed upon the earth so tenderly and neat.
Just our house left standing, where all the ends did meet.
It wasn't a rambling, giant house, but small and low and pink.
And water traveled everywhere; the best that one could drink.
Our house settled near the end of rock and gravel pea,
To see the world come standing still, while gently coaxing me.
I'd run to window, door, and still, there's someone lost this day.
They wouldn't come this close alone, with life so far away.
Yet turn they must, and leave they will—there's nothing left to see.
Except the deer and one small house...of course, there's always me.

When I was ten years old, my life changed dramatically. As all kids my age, I enjoyed my time with friends at school and the ones who were here in our small subdivision for the summer. But when fall snuck in, and the summer chatter of my few friends was gone, life could be pretty lonely. Tinkerbell was getting older and cold air made her shiver, so most of my long walks I now made alone. Now that I was older, some of my boundaries had been lifted. I knew how far I could go down our street, and I respected that. Being by the Fox River didn't necessarily mean I could be in it alone, especially as the current was very fast toward the changing of the seasons. The different leaves from oak, maple, and birch trees had begun to change their colors and fall slowly to the ground. I knew that this was the time of the year when hunters would be out, so I wore a bright orange jacket and hat.

I never strayed too far, as the beauty of this place was all that I seemed to need. I liked to look for broken clamshells that would wash up along the river shore, among the algae and rocks. It seemed that every day, the Fox River would wash up some sort of treasure that would wait patiently for me to come and add to my ever-growing collection. One day, I squatted down to grab a colorful shell and happened to glance away from the river. There I saw what appeared to be paw prints. I immediately looked around me, as I thought it could be a wolf—but then I laughed at myself as I realized that it was most likely leftover prints from when Peggy Walker had let her big lab, Little Fella, out to run here a few days earlier. Something about the prints, though, made me think that there might be a lost dog somewhere. So I decided to leave the cookie that I had brought with me where the prints were, and come back tomorrow to see if the cookie was gone. Walking back, I had to go past a very dense part of the forest by the creek. I felt like I was being watched, even though I couldn't see anyone or anything in there.

I hurried home, not looking back or even breathing for that matter until I was safely in the front door and it was shut. Grandpa was sitting in his chair doing a crossword puzzle. He looked up at me and said, "What's the matter, Margie? You look like you saw a ghost."

I caught my breath and told him what I discovered and how I felt that someone or something was following me.

"Well, your instinct is pretty good," he said. "I think that you should be careful and maybe stay away from the river until whatever it is passes through the area. If you don't feed it, it won't hang around."

My heart sank—I had forgotten to tell him that I'd left my cookie there for it. I decided not to say anything and wait a day or two and then venture back down to the river. I wasn't going to be afraid to enjoy a place that I knew better than most adults just because of a lost dog.

Laughing at my own insecurities, the whole thing was soon forgotten as we settled down for a night of good shows on the TV. Routine is a funny thing. It's comfortable and safe, and even as children we cling to the routine that has been given to us. I hungered for adventure but thought better of it once it came and stared me in the face.

That night as I went to sleep, I thought I heard a wolf howling. My little dog Tinker, who had grown somewhat deaf, raised her head and listened, then shook a bit and went back to sleep. It was like she was saying, "It's not a wolf, it's just some poor lost dog out there somewhere."

I followed her example and closed my eyes and fell asleep. All was forgotten—I was worrying about something that most likely was not a threat to us anyway. A week passed, and we had a frost. It was very early in the year for that, and I was concerned that we would miss our "Indian summer," as my grandparents called it. Grandpa and I had walked to the river and hadn't seen any more prints or evidence that there was a lost dog or a stray wolf, so I felt it was safe for me to adventure once again on my own. I was surprised that Grandpa hadn't pulled our pier in yet, but he said that we still had warm fall weather to go through, and maybe Uncle Earl would be out with his boat for one more ride before the river began to freeze.

Grandpa decided to go up to the house and grab his pole. I stretched out on the pier, looking out at how high the water was and how fast it was moving, pushing against our old pier. Sometimes it pushed so hard that I felt like I was floating down the river on the pier all by myself. I spread my arms out as I lay face down, and it felt like I was flying low over the water. Getting bored, I began to jump up and down to see if I could get the pier to submerge a bit. This was a huge mistake, because part of the pier broke through, and I was in the water faster than a rock could fall. The water was so cold that it took my breath away. The clothes I was wearing became twice as heavy and made it hard to get free of the current and onto the shore. My back was to the shore. I tried to push myself away from the pier and the oncoming current, but I seemed to be stuck. I was afraid that if Grandpa didn't get back soon, I wouldn't be able to hang on any longer and would be swept down the river toward the bridge. *Why, oh, why did I jump on the pier?* My legs began to get numb, and I felt sleepy and slow. Thoughts mixed with fear raced through my body. I looked toward the shore but still saw no sign of Grandpa. I called out, but my voice was getting weak and most likely would not be heard over the wind and rushing water. Just as I decided that maybe I should not fight the current, I felt something warm at the back of my neck. It wasn't talking, but it pulled me by my collar out back toward the shore.

"Who is it?" I screamed. "Is that you, Grandpa?"

There was no reply except for a steady huffing of warm breath on the back of my neck. Whoever or whatever it was, it was strong enough to pull me and all my weighted-down clothes safely to the shore. I fell back onto the sand on my back, all wet and shivering. Then I looked up toward my forehead, and I saw the distinct features of a very large animal. Was it a bear getting ready to eat me? Was it a wolf saving me, only to attack? Gathering my strength and nerve, I sat up and turned around. I was nose-to-nose with the biggest, reddest, wolf-looking dog I had ever seen. Our noses touched, our eyes met, and all of a sudden he kissed me right on the mouth! I jumped and squealed just as my grandfather saw what was happening and started running as fast as he could, waving his hands to scare the beast away. Grandpa obviously was trying to protect me, thinking that this wolf had attacked me, but I knew better.

"Stop running, Grandpa. I'm all right, and this big guy saved me!" Grandpa stopped, and the dog wagged his tail. I explained the stupid thing I had done and how this wonderful dog had saved me.

"Well, I guess you just had another one of those life lessons, huh, Margie?" Grandpa stooped down and began to pet the dog. "You sure are lucky," he said to me while petting the dog.

"That's it!" I yelled so loud that both the dog and Grandpa jumped back. "I am going to call him Lucky!"

Grandpa knew that I was implying that we'd keep the dog. He argued at first, saying that we had no room and that Tinkerbell might not like him and that big dogs leave big poop compared to Tinkerbell's little mess...but there was no getting me to back down on this one. This dog had saved my life, and as far as I was concerned, he was staying with us.

Grandpa finally relented, and we agreed to make him a bed in the garage near the heater so he could live with us as an outdoor dog. I was so tired and cold, but I found the strength I needed to walk back to our little pink house. Lucky came next to me and allowed me to lean on him as I walked between him and Grandpa. Lucky and I went into the garage, and Grandpa closed the garage door behind us. Tinker was barking, and Grandma's teeth almost fell out when she saw me all wet and shivering, standing in her kitchen.

"Get your wet clothes off and into the tub with you," Grandma hollered. "Bill, grab the Epsom's salts and pour a cup in the tub for her to soak in. And make her one of your hot toddies to drink or she will be sick, I am sure of it." All of a sudden there was a low howl from the garage and Tinker and Grandma both stopped their chattering and listened.

Grandma looked at Grandpa, who simply said, "We have a visitor for a spell, Cleo. He saved Margie's life, and well, he needs a place to stay for a while."

I held my breath as I shook all over. Grandma nodded her head in approval and Tinkerbell gave in also. After getting bathed and drinking Grandpa's horrible concoction, I tried to sleep, but I could hear Lucky pacing back and forth in the garage. Grandpa went into the garage and left the back door open a crack. I watched as Lucky bounded through the tall grass and into the woods. After a while, Grandpa came back in and sat down to work his crossword puzzle.

I whispered, "Do you think he will be back?"

Still studying his crossword, Grandpa said, "Don't know. He's a wild one, he is. I left the door open with food in a bowl. We'll see if he does or not."

I fell asleep and dreamt of my ordeal. I thought I could feel Lucky's warm breath on my neck. It made me shake, and in a foggy state, I could see Grandpa putting another blanket on me. I do not remember much after that. The next morning I woke up to a scratching sound and realized that Lucky was back. I was so happy!

Grandpa said, "We have to let Tinker out. She can hold her own, I think." For a moment I thought that Lucky would hurt her, but Tinkerbell was a tough old dog and went right out and sniffed him as he sniffed her. I looked out the door, and there they went, running around together. It seemed that we would have a good time with this new addition to our family. Tinker seemed to like the big fella, and when she chased him, he would run with his tail between his legs, looking back all the while he escaped. It was really funny to watch.

Fall became warm on the last day, and then all of a sudden it was gone. The trees were bare, the sky was gray, and we were in winter. One day in the middle of winter, Grandpa got up and went to let Lucky out of the garage, but then he came back in and asked if I had let him out already.

"Nope, not me," I said. We knew Grandma hadn't either, so we couldn't figure out how he got out. We didn't worry too much—he was an outside dog that liked to hunt and run and nose around in different parts of the woods. But then hours went by, and no matter how much I called or used the dog whistle that Grandpa gave me, Lucky didn't return. I was so very sad. Each evening I put fresh food out for him, and each morning I would have to throw it out as he didn't return. After about a month, I finally accepted the fact that he wasn't coming back at all.

I was so sad. The house was quiet. Tinker would run from the red living room chair to Grandpa's bed to look for her lost friend. One day, I was sitting with my grandparents in the front room and we started to talk about how some things change and some stay the same.

"Why do you think he left us? We gave him food and warmth, and he had all of us who loved him." I really fought the tears and felt so overcome with emotion that I had to go put my head on Grandma's lap for comfort.

Grandpa sat for a few minutes and then said, "Margie, there are people or beings like Lucky who come into our lives to help us when we need it the most. Lucky was lost, and then he found you and saved your life. Maybe that's what he was supposed to do, and even though he isn't here with us in the physical sense any more, he will always be with us in the spiritual sense."

That didn't make me feel any better, and I cried myself through supper. Later that night as I was waiting for Tinkerbell to come back in, I thought I heard a dog panting. I looked around but saw nothing there. Standing still, I could still feel the warm lick on my nose when Lucky saved me from drowning. Tinkerbell went off running around the side of the house. I yelled at her to come back, but before I knew it, she was in the deepest part thicket that ran alongside of the creek. I followed her in, figuring that she had seen a rabbit. And then I stopped in my tracks as I saw Lucky. Tinker came back and jumped into my arms while I stood there looking at him. Lucky looked so dirty, and he was thinner. I reached out my hand to offer him some food, but he backed away. After what seemed like an eternity, he turned away and was gone. That was the last time I saw Lucky. When I told my grandparents through my tears, there were no words that could comfort me.

That night when I went to kiss my grandmother good-night, she grabbed my hand and said, "We all come and go like the wind or a shooting star. Life is not sad if you allow the good to seep in. Think of what that dog did for you, and then let him go. We aren't going to be here forever either, ya know."

Well, that comment hit me hard, and I swore up and down through my tears and gasping breaths that when and if they died, I would die on the same day and that I would take Tinker with me.

Of course that didn't happen. Life went on, and I left Colby Point and the life I had with my grandparents the following year. I went to live with my mother and stepfather in Chicago. As we drove away from that little pink house at the end of the gravel road, I tried to take mental pictures so I would not forget anything, ever!

My grandparents waved to me as we drove away. And then, out of the corner of my eye, I saw him standing at the edge of the field. It was Lucky, and he was running after us as we turned the corner. Of course he couldn't catch up. I decided to say nothing to my parents, because I knew the city was not a good place for a dog like him. No matter how hard I tried to convince myself, my grandparents' words rang in my ears. I knew that they were right.

Grandpa Bill and Grandma Cleo had taught me the best that they could. Grandma's words played over and over in my head: "People come and go, as do the other beings in our lives. What we choose to remember and use and hang onto is what makes us the people we are today."

My grandparents taught me, Lucky saved me, and the Fox...well, it simply took me away.

EPILOGUE

Night Train

There is a sound that I can hear when I am still asleep
Wherever my dreams take me, pulling me out from the deep
This sound, a lonely haunting wail, it always sounds the same
Back into my childhood days and the calm of the night train.
Once awake I rub my lids and focus tired eyes
My thoughts go towards the night train, and the lights beneath the sky
I wonder of the sights it sees, the voices that it's heard
The night train has a bond with them of no unspoken words
The train is prodding, pressing, pleading, urging me to run
My spirit that's within the orb has slowly come undone
And while I lay here lazily, hazily in vain
The single most secluded sound, the tempting midnight train.

∽

I wrote that poem while lying in bed one evening, thinking about my grandparents. Grandpa was slow and sweet and somewhat confused. Grandma, although still sharp in her mind, was ravaged by her disease that began to break down her body in the worst ways.

I'd been married for two years, and Dan and I had our first son, Danny. All I could think of was the beauty of Colby Point and the wonderful people who had taken such good care of me at one time. I knew they needed my help now. I knew we had to move back home. It wasn't going to be easy as Grandpa had his room and Grandma had her room and there was only an old foldout couch in the living room for Dan and me. Danny's small crib would fit there, too. It would be tight but it would work—we had to do it. I would care for my grandparents in the last part of their lives like they had cared for me at the beginning of mine.

We went ahead and moved, and I settled down into a routine, as did my husband. He left each morning for the long, thirty-mile drive to work. I'd watch him leave me at the end of the road, and then I would take my baby and sit in Grandma's room. I'd settle down and nurse him while we talked. It was like the years fell away, and I was that young girl playing dolls again while Grandma told me stories. Each morning was the same, and I thoroughly enjoyed it. It was hectic some days, as sometimes Grandpa would forget what he was supposed to be doing and Tinkerbell (yes, she was still alive) would begin to bark at ghosts in the air.

All in all I was happy to be with them, and everything that had seemed so magical when I was little still had a mystery waiting to unfold. I cooked for them, kept the small home clean, and did the shopping. Routine was important to them, and it actually helped me with my care of my son. Being a young mother with no real modern conveniences of the day was a bit frustrating, but from my grandmother came the easy knowledge that whatever was wrong always worked its way out, usually for the better.

I began to view my life in this house as a preparation of sorts, so that I would be able to instill the same values in my children that my grandparents had instilled in me. After my sons (four of them) were grown, and my grandparents and Tinker had passed away, I made the decision to sell the old home.

I carefully went through the household items and decided to have a yard sale. It was actually funny—we lived about seventeen miles from the nearest big town, so I thought no one would really come to a little house at the end of the road. I was surprised though, and before I knew it, most of the furniture and dishes and memories were living with other people.

I wish I would have stopped and not have been so eager for change. I miss Grandma Cleo's English blue dishes and her yellow cake bowl. If I could only open up Grandpa Bill's toolbox one more time and feel the cool, smooth tools in my hands.... Why was I so anxious to leave behind all those things that helped shape me? But I remembered them, and told each story to my kids who listened and enjoyed them and asked for more. Then I got to share them with my grandchildren. Watching their eyes light up and seeing the anticipation on their faces while I told my stories brought all the magic back to me!

I want to say that every single story in this book is true as I remember it. These things happened to me—Margie. I saw my grandfather save a wounded dear and I witnessed the kindness of a stranger on a cold winter's night and then saw him disappear. The circle creek really did flow in circles, and the sweetest time was when I was sprayed in the face with chocolate as they pulled Carrie Medlinger out of the old well. I wrote these stories down because I want to make sure that they are around to be shared with the ones you love. Each story is about hope and faith and, of course, magic!

Anyway, getting back to my poem—as I said, I wrote it one night while in bed. I had had a particularly hard day with my kids and my grandparents who had suddenly become my children. I wished for a different life, one alone and free. I never was alone in my life, and I wondered what it would be like to be on that train, escaping... if only for a moment. It was a guilty pleasure, and one that I hid for quite a while. I was ashamed and blushed after I wrote my poem and almost threw it away. But as life progressed, I realized that my stories and my words were going to save me. I find myself falling back to the very thought of them waltzing through my dreams at night. These memories have brought the sweetness back to an otherwise difficult life.

When faced with a future that seems to be at a standstill, the best thing we can do is to revisit our past. There are so many things to learn from the past, which can change the future we have now. I have learned that recently, and as I learn from the events of my life, the future is so very bright.

Thank you, Cleo and Bill Mauer, for the very thought of you... my love.